Lu

The Vocational Cal...

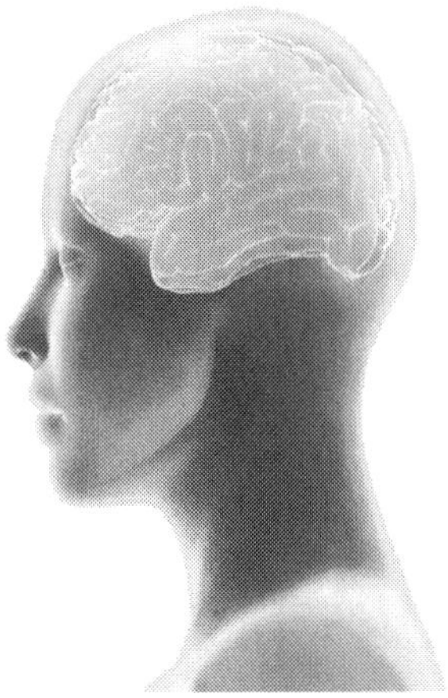

Luca Rohleder

The Vocational Calling for Highly Sensitive Persons

The Fine Line Between Brilliance and Burnout

dielus

Where links to third-party websites occur in this book, no ownership or liability is assumed. These links refer solely to their status at the time of publication.

This book is also available as an e-book, ISBN 978-3-9823032-3-9.

The Vocational Calling for Highly Sensitive Persons

Author: Luca Rohleder

English translation: Dr. Cynthia Dyre

Publishing company: dielus edition; Weißenfelser Str. 15, 04229 Leipzig, Germany

Based on: Die Berufung für Hochsensible, Luca Rohleder (german edition)

This book has been published by an independent publishing house. The publisher affirms that no international investor groups, major publishers or other corporations have had any involvement in the book. The content of this guide is based exclusively on independent, expertise-based criteria.

Images: ©iStock.com/janulla (Head)
©iStock.com/Ola_Tarakanova (Butterflies)

ISBN-13: 978-3-9823032-2-2

ISBN-10: 3-9823032-2-2

Bibliographic information from the German National Library: The German National Library lists this publication in the German National Bibliography; detailed bibliographic data are available on the Internet at https://portal.d-nb.de.

AUTHOR'S NOTE

This book differs from conventional self-help guides in that high sensitivity is not a scientifically recognized personality trait.

Any claim to have written a scientific study of the subject would therefore be a contradiction in terms. This will, incidentally, most likely also remain the case going forward, since in research and research publications on high sensitivity, the issue of self-diagnosis or self-attribution on the part of study participants or respondents cannot be resolved.

For this reason, this work presents a complementary psychological model as an approach to understanding high sensitivity. Additional major portions of the book are based on empirically proven data as well as on the ability to intuitively understand complex interrelationships.

Finally, it should be noted that this book is not intended as an instruction manual for self-treatment. Anyone experiencing psychological impairment is advised to seek professional help.

„Letting go means having the courage
to surrender tomorrow to its own destiny.“

Luca Rohleder

TABLE OF CONTENTS

FOREWORD

This English translation is based on the latest edition of the German best-seller *Die Berufung für Hochsensible* and therefore reflects the most current information available.

Originally, my book was one of the very first on the topic of the highly sensitive person to appear in the German language. The idea for the original manuscript arose in the early 2010s, at a time when only a handful of authors had begun to write about the topic. *Elaine Aron's* standard work *The Highly Sensitive Person* had served to generate interest in the subject. Her best-seller, the German translation of which was eventually published in the mid-2000s, not only gave birth to the term "highly sensitive," but provided a comprehensive definition of it. In my subsequently published book, I therefore followed, to the greatest extent possible, *Elaine Aron's* definition of high sensitivity.

The term "highly sensitive person" customarily appears as the acronym "HSP." I have used this abbreviation throughout this book as well.

Beyond this, I would also like to take this opportunity to thank the many people who have already read this book. It is only thanks to them that this book has attained a total circulation in the six figures. This not only brought early awareness to a broad public of the issues facing highly sensitive people but has also inspired many other experts and authors to delve into the topic more deeply.

You may be wondering if you yourself are indeed a highly sensitive person. I can assure you that once you have read this book, you will have a definitive answer to that question. In any case, there is no doubt that this topic somehow relates to you – books have a way of appearing at the right time in the right place. At the very least, you have likely been confronted with the concept of high sensitivity, if not in connection with yourself personally, then through others in your closest professional or private circles.

It is most often the HSPs among us who experience the greatest difficulties in their professional lives. When it comes to our degree of social integration, our self-image, and our daily routines, our jobs are the decisive factor in determining these. Our professional lives have an enormous influence on our overall well-being. If things aren't going well at the workplace, then things aren't going well for us anywhere else. We may even lose sleep over this, meaning that we are then confronted with these problems twenty-four hours a day. If all of this escalates into looming existential fears, our jobs may even endanger our health.

As a result of all this, people tended to only come to me for help when things had already reached a boiling point – their problems had reached crisis state. This is simply human nature; in general, we don't call for an expert until the damage is almost done. This is when I would encounter employees who were in a state of absolute desperation, and they were quick to discuss the major existential issues they faced.

This meant that most of the people who came to me for help were already experiencing a psychological crisis. Over the years, I have been confronted with the entire spectrum of psychological conditions, which has often led me to walk a fine line between offering specific work-related advice or life guidance.

These days, unfortunately, I have less and less time to devote to my work as a coach and trainer. I see the focus of my current work more as that of enlightenment. I also want to spend more time promoting the topic of high sensitivity among young experts, which is why, several years ago, I established one of the largest networks for highly sensitive people in the German-speaking world.

I nevertheless look back on a career that spanned more than two decades. I can usually tell just by looking at a job application if the person is highly sensitive. This is evidenced in the job moves, career changes, leaves of absence, sick leaves, and failed attempts at entrepreneurship. Being constantly on the search for something new is one of the typical signs of a highly sensitive person. This has caused some people so much anguish that they felt compelled to pursue psychological counseling.

The aim of this guide is to stop that process before it even begins. I want to show HSPs that there is still much hope, if they will only learn more about the topics of *personal growth* and the *intuitively led life.* I have poured the totality of my twenty years of professional experience into this. It will become clear that there is a specific reason why people are born highly sensitive. If you look at the entire life spans of these people, you will also see that a common thread runs through them, pointing to a specific vocational calling. You need only reach out and seize it.

And so, here is what I will show you in this book: that you are indeed here to fulfill a very specific task. In the words of Martin Luther: "*The external vocation of every person is based on an internal calling.*"

If you truly are highly sensitive, you will be amazed at how unambiguously your specific vocational path is laid out before you. In writing this book, my desire is to help you to put an end to your (perhaps agonizing) search for your vocational calling.

Luca Rohleder

(www.hochsensibilitaet-netzwerk.com)

Part A

Past and Present

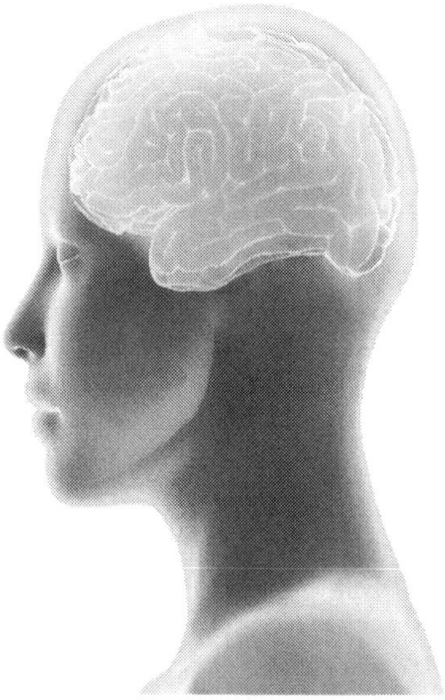

The definition of insanity is doing the same thing over and over again and expecting different results.

(Albert Einstein)

1 Why Am I Like This?

It has probably already occurred to you that throughout your entire life, you've been preoccupied with the question of "why." "Why am I like this?" "Why am I living in a world like this?" "Why can't I find the right career for me?" "Why does everyone else seem to be doing better than I am?" "Why did he just say that?" "Why does everything seem so senseless?" "Why does everybody lie?"

Why, why, why ...

To help explain what you're experiencing, I'd like to introduce a psychological model. The concept behind it is based on the idea that your ego consists of multiple ego states, and that one of these ego states represents your inner child.

The theory of the "inner child" originated from a psychological approach used to understand the internal realm of lived experiences and was made well-known through books by *John Bradshaw* and *Erika Chopich/Margaret Paul.* It is also an element in *transactional analysis*, developed by American psychiatrist *Eric Berne.*

The inner child signifies and symbolizes emotions, feelings, memories, and experiences from our childhoods. This spans the entire spectrum of intense feelings, from unbridled joy to devastating pain, including happiness and sorrow, intuition and curiosity, and feelings of abandonment, fear, and anger. The inner child encompasses everything we associate with being, feeling, and experiencing, all of which are processed by specific areas of the brain. This model presupposes an ego that is divided into an observing, reflective INNER ADULT and a sensing, experiencing INNER CHILD.

This representation of your inner psyche may initially sound a bit like pop-science, but it is actually a wonderfully intelligent approach to helping you better understand yourself. It will provide answers to your many questions of *why*. There is a slight catch, however: It is not very well suited for helping you understand your specific situation as a highly sensitive person. To be able to arrive at a thorough description of HSPs, I believe that we need to identify not just two, but rather three ego states. I'm therefore going to add in a third one: a HIGHER EGO STATE. I'm also going to replace the term "inner child" with NEWBORN EGO STATE. This will make the distinction between HSPs and non-highly sensitive people significantly clearer. Taken together, the following THREE-EGO-STATE MODEL emerges:

1. NEWBORN EGO STATE (NES)
2. HIGHER EGO STATE (HES)
3. ADULT EGO STATE (AES)

In subsequent chapters, I will provide a more detailed explanation of these terms. You will see that this THREE-EGO-STATE MODEL allows a virtually seamless professionally based identification of the traits found in highly sensitive people. Let's begin now with your first ego state.

1.1 NEWBORN EGO STATE

You are going to learn that your personal inner child is not a typical one. Instead, it displays many characteristics that we would more commonly associate with a newborn baby. To illustrate this, I'll begin with a description of the traditional philosophy of the inner child. Let's take a look at the fundamental needs of all children:

- Children need to play, run around, and have fun.
- Children need to learn and have new experiences.
- Children need social interaction, to have friends, and be loved.
- Children need to be protected and cared for.

As a rule, childhood and youth are the happiest times of our lives. Nevertheless, most of us will, sooner or later, be forced to take on the responsibilities of adulthood. At the very latest, when the time comes to start our own families, there will be new personal challenges we will have to overcome. The ADULT EGO STATE will become more and more significant. Reality steps in. We become caught up in our parental duties and new tasks determine our daily routines. What adults have (hopefully) received as children, they must now pass on to their own children:

- Adults provide their children with opportunities for play, a variety of activities, and joyful experiences.
- Adults send their children to school; they teach and nurture them.
- Adults provide their children with love and social interaction.

- Adults ensure that their children have structure, support, protection, a safe home, and financial security.

The process is now reversed. No longer the "takers," adults become the givers. As we mature into adulthood, this basic principle of human development is virtually universal. However, it isn't the case that the ADULT EGO STATE now simply takes over and replaces our childlike personality – rather, it augments it. This means that every adult still retains a certain childlikeness. We can see this in the fact that adults still have some of the same needs as children – it's just that once we reach a certain age, we describe them differently:

- Adults want to enjoy new experiences, to experiment, to be adventurous (play, have fun).
- Adults learn a profession, educate themselves further, and gain life experience (learn and experience).
- Adults seek out friends and partners; they may marry (love and social interaction).
- Adults create a home, earn money, and ensure that they have financial reserves (protection and security).

So, if you describe the general characteristics and basic needs of a child and then express these in adult terms, you arrive at the definition of the inner child. Your first ego state thus represents your own fundamental needs. Whenever you successfully satisfy these longings, you experience positive emotions.

The inner child is therefore responsible for our happiness, enjoyment of life, self-esteem, love, etc. When things go wrong, however, or if some of your emotional needs are not met, you will, unfortunately, also experience fear, sorrow, anger, disappointment, etc. The inner child represents the entire spectrum of your emotional existence.

If you were able to unerringly analyze the experiences of your earliest childhood (which has been proven by modern psychology to be impossible), this would then also provide you with information about your emotional life as an adult.

In short, if we describe the basic needs of children and then express these in adult terms, we will have identified the emotional longings of all human beings, even those who are long past infancy. So far, so good.

However, as previously mentioned, this philosophy is not completely applicable to your highly sensitive nature. In your case in particular, you will see that the best depiction of your emotional disposition is not the image of a growing child, but rather that of an infant still in the phase before, during, or shortly after birth. To be able to shed a light on the mysterious world of high sensitivity, we must first examine the basic needs of infants.

Your inner child is more like an inner infant.

For instance, newborns are not in the least interested in playmates. Nor can they run around the house or figure out what role they need to play to best fit in with their surroundings. And they have absolutely no desire to build sandcastles or even own any possessions.

The basic needs of these adorable, yet vulnerable little creatures are completely different. All they require is protection, warmth, nourishment, and someone who will lovingly care for them. Your inner child thus finds itself in a far more existential phase of life than the inner child of a non-highly sensitive person.

As already mentioned, it is expressly this distinction that my *three-ego-state model* was designed to illuminate. Throughout the rest of this book, I will exclusively refer to the emotional part of your ego as the NEWBORN EGO STATE (NES).

You may even notice physical indications that you carry this NEWBORN EGO STATE within you. After all, your external appearance is also a reflection of your inner self. It is highly probable that your eyes are still the exact same color they were at birth. In your case, your irises probably never got darker. While many newborns' eyes change color soon after birth, your eyes may have remained blue. Or perhaps you have the same thin or fair skin with which you were born. It may also be that, like a baby, you still feel the need to sleep and eat fairly often. In extreme cases, you may, deep inside, have a profound feeling that you need someone to provide for you, protect you, and care for you (just as a newborn baby does).

Perhaps your only indication is an under-developed immune system – after all, this matures only years after we are born. Or maybe you've been in a years-long, seemingly futile battle to lose your baby fat.

It could also be that your skin is baby-like: It may be so sensitive that you are practically compulsive about removing all the tags from your clothing. You may also have been one of those children who complained to their long-suffering mothers that everything itched – to the point where she no longer knew what she could buy for you to wear.

Your sensitivity may force you to keep tugging and pulling at your clothing until even the tiniest annoying wrinkle has been smoothed out. And you may constantly find yourself sliding around in your seat because your thin skin makes it impossible to find a comfortable position, or the chair is just too hard. Tight clothing or clothes that cut into your stomach or your waist may also be difficult for you to tolerate.

The same applies to those flabby little rolls on your stomach – the ones that are so small that no one else even notices them, but that drive you crazy. Because your skin is so sensitive, you are constantly aware of them. This is likely to somehow make sweatpants or loose clothing your apparel of choice.

How many typical characteristics of a newborn can you identify in yourself?

Generally speaking, the NES may manifest itself differently in every HSP. Yet, what is notable is that not only is the skin hypersensitive, but so is – and especially so – the abdominal area. After all, this is the region of the body that is associated with our entire emotional spectrum. Of course, it is also associated with everything related to how we process the food we eat. It stands to reason that for us to be able to determine what is filling up our bellies, our sensory organs need to be highly developed. It may therefore be that you have excellent vision, a strong sense of smell, extremely sensitive hearing or sense of touch, or highly sensitive taste buds.

Even memories of your time in your mother's womb play an important role for you, at least on a subliminal level. The comfort and security you felt as you lingered in that protective and nurturing environment are something you may still be seeking to recreate – perhaps by sitting on a soft sofa, wrapped up in a warm cuddly blanket. If, while doing so, you are also enjoying some culinary treats in the comfort of your own beautifully furnished home, then this situation comes quite close to recreating what you imagine those ideal moments to have been.

Something else you may do, however, is that as you are falling asleep, you pull yourself into a typical fetal position.

Basically, you've never stopped longing for the security you felt in the womb. Perhaps the world you encountered during your birth has seemed, from the beginning, to be too cold and too dangerous. If so, you then determined that you would remain a newborn, so that you would never be too far away from your protective mother.

Even later, as you became an adolescent, you couldn't shake the feeling that you were somehow not adequately equipped to handle the harshness of reality. Even when you were surrounded by people your own age, you had the feeling that you were somehow smaller, more vulnerable, or simply different. Perhaps your peers even seemed like strangers to you. And this literally compelled you to ask yourself over and over again whether you even belonged to this world. You never felt you were on the same page as others. It may also be that your childhood consisted only of "fight or flight" moments or that you decided to remain a loner.

All in all, the presence of a NEWBORN EGO STATE constitutes a special challenge. It usually manifests itself in physical and emotional sensitivities, frequent conflicts with reality, and a great deal of personal drama. In this book, I will discuss these topics in greater detail as well.

If you feel that you, too, because of your high sensitivity, are confronted by these kinds of challenges, please don't think that the fates have somehow betrayed you.

Your NEWBORN EGO STATE
has a deeper significance.

The very fact that you carry within yourself not just a conventional inner child, but a super-sensitive NEWBORN EGO STATE, is the one essential factor that allows a vital trait of your being to emerge. This makes you a very special person.

1.2 HIGHER EGO STATE

Your inner child is still at the developmental stage of a newborn – the effects of this character extreme will be the decisive factor in your vocational calling.

Even though your initial reaction may be that this all sounds somewhat demeaning, the fact that you possess an NES means that you still retain a strong connection to the greater whole. You essentially have a direct link to a subtle source of information. This source is known by many different names. You may call it higher knowledge, instinct, guardian angel, God, soul, gut feeling, or something else entirely (completely in line with your personal beliefs). Throughout this book, I myself will refer to all of this as your INTUITION.

I haven't selected the term HIGHER EGO STATE here to indicate that you live in some sort of lofty, detached world, but because your instinct/intuition operates on a fundamentally higher level than your intellect. To put it another way, your intuition always knows better than your conscious mind. Incidentally, from an evolutionary perspective, this makes complete sense, since without their instincts, animals would never be able to survive. After all, in comparison to the most highly evolved animal, i.e., humans, they possess only minimal consciousness (depending on their evolutionary stage).

People have been arguing for millennia about exactly how our intuition actually works, so I am obviously not going to be able to present you here with some wise, conclusive answer to that question. I personally feel quite drawn to quantum mechanics and astrophysics. In these disciplines, media that our conscious minds cannot grasp are referred to as either *quantum level* or *dark matter/dark energy* (I have written a science novel on this topic: "Die Suche nach Gott" (*The Search for God*)). Of course, you don't have to agree with this physics-based perspective – there is absolutely no requirement to do so. In any explanations regarding the media your intuition accesses, I will keep the discussion quite general. My only concrete premise is that our intuition is interconnected with something not consciously perceptible to our other senses. I will simply use a universal term to refer to this mysterious source of information: the INVISIBLE WORLD. As you encounter this term, you can mentally replace or supplement it based on your own worldview, fundamental values, or even your spiritual beliefs.

Highly sensitive people still possess a direct connection to the INVISIBLE WORLD.

Your second ego state therefore consists of your HIGHER EGO STATE, which is responsible for the functioning of your intuition. In and of itself, there is nothing unique about this – it can be said about virtually every living earthly creature.

For at least a certain period after birth, all humans still have a direct connection to the INVISIBLE WORLD. Mothers who attentively observe their infants or toddlers, or listen carefully to them (once they begin to speak their first words), will become aware of these enduring primal instincts, which are accessing something we ourselves can't properly comprehend. As the child grows up, however, conscious thinking gradually and increasingly displaces this direct connection. Our actions are no longer guided by those primal instincts – our free will and intellect take control. Rather than purely following our instincts, our lives become increasingly guided by our consciously experienced minds.

However, by virtue of the fact that you are an HSP, your experience is quite different – after all, you possess an NES, not a conventional inner child. This means that in your case, your primal instincts will not necessarily completely fade away over the course of your life. What distinguishes you most from non-highly sensitive people is the fact that in your particular case, your intuitive connection has been significantly less weakened. Consequently – just as do babies – you still have access to this direct primal channel to the INVISIBLE WORLD.

HSPs retain all of their primal instincts.

You, therefore, would be able to survive in the real world even if you didn't possess consciousness, much as do the flora and fauna. Even in the absence of a highly developed cerebrum, animals and plants "know" what they must do.

HSPs have the ability to lead their lives without having to consciously think about it.

Even if your first thought is, "*This can't possibly all be true – I've driven myself crazy for ages with all the thinking I do about my life*," I can only tell you this: It is probably all for nothing.

Your skilled intuition is the single most important characteristic of your highly sensitive being. This would allow your HES, all by itself, to provide you with adequate protection and life guidance. Your outstanding ability to still retain possession of these primal instincts is, in a manner of speaking, preserved in you forever. It is an enviable gift, one that has the potential to provide you with a carefree future.

If, for example, you were out hiking in the mountains and got lost, this wouldn't be a particularly dangerous situation for you as an HSP. You would actually just need to wander around, not consciously thinking about anything, and everything would work itself out. Seemingly by chance, you would come across helpful clues or perhaps even encounter other people who would point you in the right direction. Or, as if by magic, some other form of help would appear. You, meanwhile, would think that this was all just a wonderful coincidence (*I'm so glad I ran into you – the angels must have sent you my way ...*)

You actually have the ability to put your life fully in the hands of your intuition. Your gut instincts could lead you directly into the happiest of circumstances. You could essentially find yourself in the right place at the right time, meeting the right people – and your conscious mind wouldn't have the faintest idea how all of this had happened.

Highly sensitive people have the ability to live a purely INTUITIVE LIFE.

So, whenever you make decisions without outside influence and without giving them too much thought – whenever you simply *do* something, or even simply *stop* doing something for a moment – things will work out in your favor.

Especially in dangerous situations, when your body shifts into emergency mode and your brain is at maximum attention (focused), you can rely on your intuition. This is evidenced by the fact that in these types of situations, it is always, of all people, the HSPs who suddenly emerge from their natural reservedness and take charge. Without consciously thinking about it, you almost automatically know what needs to be done in these extreme situations. It's almost as though you are operating under remote control. In cases like this, your strong HES has allowed your intuitive skills to spring into action.

It's probably now becoming clear to you why it is so extremely important to your existence that you possess an ego state that can be traced back to a newborn. While this makes you significantly more sensitive (perhaps even hypersensitive), it conversely puts you in possession of an additional, highly powerful ego state.

Without a NEWBORN EGO STATE, you would never have been able to retain all your primal instincts.

Consequently, you alone possess such an impressive personality trait. While it's true that you are carrying around a vulnerable NES, at the same time, you also possess an all-powerful HES. If you view the package as a whole, the combination is practically perfect for getting you through life safely and securely – assuming, of course, that you are also aware of this complete package.

Had you been born into an ancient culture, your true nature would likely have been recognized quite early. You would have been instructed as to how you could tap into your HES on a professional basis and thereby profit from it. And you certainly would also have been provided with food, housing, money, and other amenities. You would have been tended to and cared for so that you could later benefit from the wonderful guidance your intuition would provide.

Incidentally, your vast intuitive powers go even further: Along with your potential ability to glide seemingly magically into positive situations or lucky coincidences in life, the entire realm of wisdom, ideas, and ideals naturally also lies at your feet.

HSPs possess highly developed INTUITIVE KNOWLEDGE.

For instance, when you enter a room full of strangers, you immediately KNOW what the story is. Even though you haven't yet had a real conversation with anyone, you can intuitively and unerringly size up the situation. At the very least, you immediately recognize whether something is right or wrong. You already are conscious of some hazy information, even though no facts are yet on the table. I'm sure you've experienced this in your everyday life. This means that your HES has the potential to provide you not only with protection and guidance, but also with wisdom. I'll come back to this idea later. Before I do so, however, we need to take a brief look at your third ego state. This is the part of your personality with which you are probably most familiar.

1.3 THE ADULT EGO STATE

The third part of your personality is, in practical terms, your intellect. You could also refer to it as your consciousness or your mind.

It can sometimes be difficult to differentiate your ADULT EGO STATE from your other two ego states. After all, some of the information that arrives in your head has been initiated by your NES (*joy, fear, etc.*) and your HES (*intuition, knowledge, etc.*). So, your brain is made up of a rather diffuse brew of feelings, stimuli, processes, and actions. In other words, everything associated with the ways in which you process the information you receive through hearing, seeing, smelling, speaking, tasting, moving, etc.

When people speak of their inner selves, they are usually referring to their AES, so, for that reason, I'd like to maintain that practice in this book. When I address you directly here, I am speaking to you as your ADULT EGO STATE.

Your AES is the part of your being that is currently holding this book in their hands. You are the one who transforms the individual letters on the page into meaningful information. As you do so, you are also simultaneously able to develop a sense of your other two ego states. In the process, your NES will allow emotions to rise up in you, while at the same time, your HES will deliver the "Aha!" effect: that gut feeling, so to speak, that continuously lets you know if something is true for you, or whether something seems applicable to you. And it doesn't rely on any outside verifiable sources or other type of evidence to do this. Your intuition doesn't need any external sources – ultimately, it itself is a form of higher source.

Incidentally, although this "Aha!" effect is commonly described as a process of feeling (*I have the feeling something isn't right*), your HES is actually not the source any typical kinds of feelings, but instead provides you with genuine knowledge. Facts, insights, and certainties enter your mind and must be processed. Depending on how much practice and experience you have had in being able to differentiate intuitive knowledge from purely intellectual information, you will at the very least notice a sense that you are having a hunch or some other specific sensation. The term "gut feeling" is actually quite misleading, because what your intuition is really generating is concrete KNOWLEDGE.

What this means is that if you are experiencing specific emotions, such as joy, pleasure, desire, worry, or sorrow, these are coming from your NES, not your HES.

I know this all sounds quite complicated. But, in order for you to better understand all the rest of the information in this book, and to be sure we are speaking the same language, we need to make this precise differentiation absolutely clear.

Let's turn back to your ADULT EGO STATE: You can now see that at the exact moment you *do* something or decide *not to do* something, all kinds of things are running through your head – creating an enormous potential for inner conflict. Your highly sensitive personality is ultimately under the influence of two extremes: Your AES is confronted not only with a hypersensitive NES, but also with an all-powerful HES. Your AES therefore has a lot of input coming in and is constantly in danger of being overwhelmed.

Every second of every minute of every day, you are being pelted with nerve impulses. Added to these are messages from your NES (*I'm scared, I can't do that*). And on top of all this come the countless stimuli from your physical senses, like sight (*that doesn't look right*), hearing (*not this stupid tinnitus again!*), smell (*is there something toxic in the air here?*), touch (*this seat is too hard*), taste (*is this healthy?*), along with your muscular coordination (*this stupid neck pain!*)

Finally, your brain takes this entire mashup of thoughts and feelings, and compares, links, and processes them with memories (*I'm not buying these socks again, they always cut into my leg*) and neuroses (*that pen is not lined up exactly parallel to the edge of the table*). And of course, there are also the innumerable projections we make about the future (ideas), etc., etc., etc.

As I've said, all of this goes on in the heads of just about everyone. What differentiates you from non-highly sensitive people, however, are the extremes! First and foremost, the significantly higher volume of incoming information. Not only do you have an astoundingly extreme NES and HES, which are bombarding your brain with more nerve impulses than non-HSPs have to deal with, but you also have at least one physical sense that is hypersensitive. You can think of this as being similar to the resolution of a digital camera: the more pixels it has or that it can process and save, the higher the quality of the photos. However, this also generates exorbitant amounts of data. Your brain is basically always operating at the absolute limit of its capabilities.

HSPs must cognitively process an exorbitantly higher number of stimuli than do non-HSPs.

Now you can understand why it sometimes feels impossible for you to change gears quickly. When you are faced with a new (and potentially threatening or difficult to assess) situation, any spontaneity you may have goes out the window. The volume of data that must be processed in that moment is simply too great.

The complex thought processes HSPs must work through hinder them from acting spontaneously.

When it comes to disagreements or conflicts, it may often be hours or even days later that you come up with just the right counterargument or course of action. This makes it practically impossible for you to react quickly in situations where it is called for. But don't worry, you don't need to. Once you've gained enough experience in the INTUITIVELY LED LIFE, you won't need to think quickly or suddenly change gears. Then, it will actually suffice to simply employ a little more patience – more on this later ...

They say a picture is worth a thousand words. Close this book right now, and take a closer look at the image on the front cover.

—

It vividly illustrates the overall processing load taking place in your brain.

> Highly sensitive people are the ones whose brains are "on fire."

Claudia has been invited to a group cooking event. Upon her arrival, she notices that of the ten other people there, eight are people she has never met before.

Claudia immediately feels her blood pressure start to go up. Her heart rate accelerates, and her body temperature rises. She feels increasingly uncomfortable. At the same exact moment, her primal instincts kick in, bombarding Claudia with distinct impressions about the other people, the room, the situation in general, and the potential implications.

She accurately assesses the group. She notices the fake smiles as some of them greet her. With other people, it feels as though their inner frustrations or negative thoughts are being thrust upon her. And with still others, she senses simply ignorance and disinterest. With one couple, she knows immediately that the air is thick with unresolved relationship issues. All in all, it feels as though this powerful flood of information is literally going to make her head explode. A single thought goes round and round in her head: "What do I do now?" The evening hasn't even yet gotten off to a proper start, but she already feels just one deep desire: "I have to get out of here!"

That won't be possible, though, because, ultimately, Claudia has been brought up to be polite, and she doesn't want to make a bad impression. She puts her best foot forward, all the while continuing to be bombarded by a rush of information (which likely continues to upset her). Her sole occupation now is to process, evaluate, and create rational connections out of all of these myriad impressions. And then, the "have to's" make their appearance: "I have to say something, I have to smile now, I have to be funny," etc.

But what actually ends up happening is exactly the opposite. The volume of incoming data slowly pushes her brain to its maximum capacity. Claudia completely loses any semblance of authenticity. Her demeanor is anything but charming. Some of the others stop paying any attention to her, which she notices immediately, of course – past experience allows her to recognize this only too well. Unhappy memories begin to stir up inside her. Still, she continues to do her best to make a good impression. Now, though, her brain is completely preoccupied with simply helping her maintain control. Claudia's behavior becomes less and less spontaneous and a vague feeling of dread comes over her.

Claudia isn't about to give up, though. After all, she's learned that her brain can handle pressure even when it is pushed far beyond the point of comfort. After three hours, however, she is completely exhausted. Now, her only thought is how to justify to the others her impending flight from this situation. Feelings of guilt nag at her, though, because what she is really doing is attempting to come up with a little white lie.

The moment finally arrives. An absolute worst-case scenario. Out of nowhere, Claudia suddenly blurts out: "I'm afraid I have to go now – my babysitter can only stay until 11:00." She literally jumps up from the table, leaving the puzzled faces of the others behind. She flees the tortuous scene.

In reality, nothing horrible has occurred. But Claudia is at the end of her rope. Once she arrives home, she is quickly able to relax though, grateful to be back in her safe haven. The first thing she does is pour herself a glass of red wine to help her wind down more quickly. The alcohol fulfills its intended purpose. As Claudia's brain cells begin to be destroyed, the functioning of her over-stimulated mind slows. She begins to feel at ease again.

Claudia is now able to calmly take stock of the events of the evening. She gradually begins to detest herself for her ridiculous behavior. As she has done repeatedly in the past, she tells herself: "There is something wrong with me."

This sort of abrupt disappearing act must sound familiar to you – perhaps you've even fled the scene yourself without saying goodbye. But, in situations like this, it is absolutely the right thing to do. If your *red-hot* brain is on the verge of bursting into flame, it's time to call in the neuronal fire department. You have to immediately block the incoming flood of stimuli.

You've probably never actually been aware of what's going on in your head when all of this happens. You also may not have realized that you are constantly having to process the feelings and moods of other people. Ultimately, your strong intuitive powers also make you highly empathetic. And this means that, like it or not, you are going be affected by everything around you. You will rarely be able prevent this from happening, because your strong HES literally forces you to deal with the dirty laundry of all the other people around you.

HSPs not only take in external information about their surroundings, but, as if handed it on a silver platter, are also the recipients of subliminal information.

You are surely familiar with this phenomenon – at the very least, from your childhood days. Even back then, you were able to see right through your parents and other relatives. Early on, you were able sense a lot of the hypocrisy behind their facades. You may also have experienced some greatly unhappy moments in which you realized that they simply found you annoying. And if, instead of providing you with love, your mother demanded it from you, you will also have recognized this terrible, aberrant situation.

You actually never had a choice. As I noted above – it's as though all this information is being handed to you on a silver platter. And if your parents were perhaps not strong enough themselves to be able to protect you enough emotionally, you will have sensed this more intensely than you ever desired.

In the end, you were confronted at far too young an age with the full spectrum of reality. From the beginning, life placed a special burden on you. Basically, while you were still a child, you encountered the true nature of human beings in all of its facets, which are definitely not all positive. Ignorance is bliss – but even as a child, you were, unfortunately, anything but ignorant.

This may be the greatest challenge of your highly sensitive life. You are in constant danger of seeing only the negative aspects of the people around you. Only as you go through life will you realize that there are also ample positive aspects. It's just a question of what you choose to focus on.

As a separate issue, human beings are, of course, at the top of the food chain. There is only one explanation for this evolutionary achievement: Humans were able to gain this exceptional evolutionary advantage over all other living beings only because they have the greatest will to survive. It could also be said that humans are by far the most aggressive creatures on earth. In Nature's pitiless game of "eat or be eaten," humans have thus far been the most successful players.

As you KNOW, of course, this fundamental law of nature – live and let die – still applies today. The only evolutionary difference is that – especially in the case of civilized society – we no longer wish to use physical violence to achieve our goals. We would greatly prefer to remain blissfully unaware of the beast that resides within us. Today's humans therefore employ far more subtle tools to assuage their persistent, undiminished levels of aggression.

What this means is that although civilized societies now take a negative view of physical violence, they have, at the same time, come up with a shrewder solution. The inhabitants of the northern hemisphere, in particular, have simply replaced *physical* abuse with *psychological* abuse. The industrialized nations have merely turned to more intellectual forms of abuse for acting out their more sinister inclinations. They have even changed the laws regarding violence so that only *physical* abuse is punishable under the law, whereas *psychological* abuse, such as belittling, excluding, humiliating, disrespecting, shaming, or other types of emotional injury are generally not subject to any form of legal retribution. But there is really no difference. Whether someone attacks you on a physical level or a psychological level, it is still an act of violence. In some cases, it might result in immediate death, and in others, death may only come on gradually. Over the course of thousands of years of evolution, nothing has changed. The beast within us is still alive and well. The weapons it employs are just more devious than they were a thousand years ago.

As an HSP, you are certainly conscious of these more disturbing aspects of life. In contrast to people who aren't highly sensitive – who would dismiss all of this as absurd – you KNOW, based on your intuition, that every human being truly has a dark side. In extreme cases, you may even come to the conclusion that *everything is simply deception and betrayal.* I personally would immediately understand what you meant by that. People who are not highly sensitive, however, wouldn't even have a clue what you were talking about. They would be absolutely non-plussed – and would have serious concerns about your psychological well-being.

As a result, over the course of your life, you have probably come up with some self-protective strategies. From a young age, you became accustomed to remaining constantly on alert, and this allowed you to quickly realize that a thick emotional protective wall could keep you safe. You also began early in life to train your powers of observation, since, after all, you had to constantly monitor your surroundings for threats.

Gradually, over time, you trained your mind to be able to make a razor-sharp analysis of a situation. Throughout your life, you have learned to take every possible threatening scenario into consideration. And today, your thought processes automatically take into account a vast range of innumerable factors, including even the most improbable scenarios. All in all, you have brought your brain's cognitive abilities to their highest level. After all those years of intensive (and involuntary) training, you are now intellectually armed to the teeth. The danger now is that you will continue to focus on your mental strengths (*and allow your brain to continue to burn red-hot*).

It would be much more expedient if you were to stop pushing your brain to its limit – after all, it is already handling a dangerously high load. It would be far better for you to pay attention to something else entirely:

The task facing highly sensitive people is to tap more intensively into their emotional realm.

A far better life strategy would be to force yourself to come into contact with a large number of other people, because this would allow you to increase your resilience (emotional resistance).

For most HSPs, however, this will sound extremely exhausting and unpleasant, and so they will go out of their way to avoid it, which puts their NES at great risk of demise. They are then left with only their intellect, which leads to the ADULT EGO STATE taking on a disproportionately large role. At this point, life begins to become too cerebral. The usual tragic result of this is a lack of grounding, purpose, and authenticity, along with the inability for self-love – not to mention an overload syndrome that may, like the sword of Damocles, hang over their heads for the rest of their lives.

You, on the other hand, can – right this very minute – take the wiser route. There is no need for you to keep boosting your mental abilities – your mind is already operating at a record-breakingly high level.

HSPs must protect their minds from persistent stress.

Your brain is like a Formula 1 racecar. These vehicles are designed to be capable of delivering top-level performance – but only for a relatively short period of time. If, on the other hand, you decided it would be a good idea to use your amazing racecar to compete in a desert rally (or even just to drive it to the grocery store every day), your exceptional Formula 1 racecar would soon be reduced to a pile of junk.

It's the same with your brain. If you don't treat it with great care, your AES – in other words, your mind – will very quickly suffer damage (more on this later). Your unnaturally strong intellectual powers generate an enormous concentration of energy in your head. If you push them to their limit or beyond, or if there is never any downtime, this can quickly lead to health problems. It's similar to the energy produced by the sun: at the appropriate strength, its rays create and sustain life. When they become too strong, they have the ability to kill.

1.4 PUTTING IT ALL TOGETHER

You will, of course, be able to find a psychiatrist, psychologist, or therapist who will tell you that you must indeed have experienced a traumatic event before, during, or shortly after your birth.

All sorts of assumptions and speculation will be brought into play: Your father or mother must surely have left you alone at home for hours. No one would have been there to hear your cries and, as a newborn, you would surely have had the feeling that you had been abandoned and left to your fate – you may even have felt that you would starve to death. Or something perfectly harmless may have happened in the hospital, but from your subjective newborn perspective, this was interpreted as a life-threatening event. The floodgates to all kinds of misunderstandings will be flung open.

Consider carefully whether it really makes sense to revisit the past.

This knowledge will rarely be helpful, especially if it serves to plant the terrible thought in your head that your mother or father could bear some responsibility for the problematic situation in which you currently find yourself. I would expressly warn you not to entertain these types of suspicions (something trained psychologists routinely engage in). I have seen this lead to dramatic familial crises, from which the family was never able to heal. As you read this book, you will learn that for you, as a highly sensitive person, feelings of resentment can have an especially detrimental effect.

It's far more critical that you remember that the fact that you possess a special NEWBORN EGO STATE rather than a conventional inner child is of fundamental importance for you. This is the underlying factor that has allowed you to retain your primal instincts, and these provide you with the most powerful weapon that exists: your intuition – your omniscience.

The materialization of such a breath-taking gift is unique, and in the end, presents you with far more advantages than disadvantages in life. It's just a question of becoming aware of it.

The problems we experience in life aren't the result of something bad that has happened to us – they are due to our lack of awareness of our own strengths and our subsequent inability to tap into these.

Even in cases, though, where the reality of the current situation is not – or cannot be – seen or accepted, conflicts can still arise. More on this later ...

To close this first chapter, I would like to point out something critical: The division of your being into three ego states is, naturally, merely a psychological model. In virtually every scientific discipline, it is accepted that instruction will be based on models, theses, or other theories. Take, for instance, Bohr's model of the atom, which we are taught in school, but which has precious little to do with the true fundamental nature of atoms. Or take the thesis from neurological research that it is our minds alone that determine who we are, although there is plenty of scientific evidence to the contrary.

Despite our innumerable models, theses, and basic scientific assumptions, we will probably never truly or fully understand how life actually functions (even if you find yourself spending a lot of time ruminating about it). But the *three-ego-state model* I have developed is wonderfully well-suited for use in a professionally based approach to identifying the special features of your personality. I was quite literally compelled to come up with something new. For one thing, my own intuition led me in a quite amazing way to this knowledge and, for another, it is based on empirical evidence from my many years of hands-on professional experience. Not to mention the fact that in academic research circles, the existence of highly sensitive character traits is being questioned, with a tendency to view high sensitivity as a pathology.

High sensitivity is a personality trait –
not a mental illness!

There is no need for concern, however. When it comes to how we regulate our lives, many of today's scientists believe that it is our *enteric nervous system*, i.e., our subconscious gut-brain, that is running the show (see, e.g., *Michael Gershon: The Second Brain*). This is taken into account in my *three-ego-state model*, since it is our gut feelings, after all, that make it possible for us to live an INTUITIVELY LED LIFE. And you, in particular, as an HSP, can become a master at this.

And yet, we are still faced with a dilemma. Even today, scientists have not found a plausible explanation for the fact that some people are able to quite quickly and easily deal with personal and psychological problems while others have an unbelievably difficult time doing so. Or why some individuals are plagued by horrific problems all their lives while fate seems to have smiled on others.

Physicians and psychologists also have no explanation for why so many people today suffer from chronic pain for which there does not appear to be an underlying reason. The same goes for addiction, obesity, and depression. And yet, other people live their entire lives without experiencing any of these problems.

Unfortunately, highly sensitive people are also among those caught up in this general confusion. Many of them spend their lives constantly searching – they undertake a journey to seek out the purpose behind everything. Some people pursue their internal and external searches to the point of sheer exhaustion.

Whether or not you are coping well with your highly sensitive personality, my model will certainly provide you with some answers. The first one has already been revealed in this chapter:

Highly sensitive people are intermediaries between the VISIBLE and the INVISIBLE WORLD.

More so than for others, you, as an HSP, are capable of tuning in directly to the realm of intuition. Even if this connection doesn't seem to be functioning quite properly right now, one thing is certain: you are dealing with a set of extremes!

At one end of the spectrum, you are as vulnerable as a newborn, and on the other, you possess almost magical intuitive powers. And, right in the middle of the spectrum, there you stand with your AES – which is most likely completely overwhelmed in its constant agonizing attempt to somehow process all of the information your mind is taking in.

You will see that, at first, these three ego states are going to generate some conflict. You will be confronted with seemingly mutually incompatible needs. When you allow one aspect of your personality to predominate, you will simultaneously be suppressing another. If you satisfy one need, it will appear as though this makes fulfilling a different desire impossible.

It's time to put an end to all of this potential drama and these apparent contradictions. In the first step, you'll become aware of the types of career paths that are best suited to your highly sensitive nature.

2 What Gifts Lie Dormant Within Me?

This topic is of such fundamental importance that, in this book, I will explicitly avoid the over-emotional undertone found in so much of the literature on high sensitivity. I'm not going to romanticize things – there is too much at stake for you. If it takes you too long to find your way, the delay can be dangerous. Your highly sensitive body isn't designed to have to permanently deal with inner conflict.

Beyond that, over the past several years, I have also had to witness too many HSPs who were literally wallowing in a kind of victim mentality. I have seen too many exceptional and, above all, highly respectable people who, in their frustration, simply vegetate in front of their televisions or numb themselves with drugs, fatty foods, or sugar. Others immerse themselves in daydreams about finding the love of their life, hoping that a new lover can help make everything right again.

To prevent yourself from slipping into any such hopeless situation, what you need, first and foremost, is *self-awareness*. As the term already implies, you can attain this by simply becoming *aware* of your*self* – and this applies above all to your many talents. That is why, in this chapter, we will address all of the hidden abilities that dwell deep within you.

Some of these you are already using – even if unconsciously – in your daily work. Others may not yet be fully developed. It depends on which phase of PERSONAL GROWTH you find yourself in. But still, you'll be surprised at just how unambiguously your strengths and gifts point you toward a very specific vocational calling. If you are highly sensitive, the following aspects will be especially applicable:

1. Knowledge
2. Independence
3. Creative Powers

Let's begin with one trait that can be an exceptional gift, but, at the same time, a burden.

2.1 KNOWLEDGE

Your exceptional intuitive abilities mean that you have a sort of divine blueprint of a perfect world in your head. This is a type of higher order that no one can really accurately define. Even you yourself will have a hard time putting it into words. It is something you simply KNOW. When you are confronted with people, situations, or circumstances, you have a perfect sense of whether things are just right or not. In a manner of speaking, you always actually know what would be ideal.

> HSPs have KNOWLEDGE of what an ideal world would look like.

You have a sixth sense for everything as to whether it is perfect or not. Your KNOWLEDGE is divided into the following aspects:

1. An understanding of harmoniousness
2. A strong conscience
3. A sense of justice

2.1.1 An Understanding of Harmoniousness

Harmoniousness is nothing more than a lofty ideal. It is the agreeable concomitance of circumstances, people, or things. Harmoniousness is another state that is difficult to grasp on an intellectual level. You have to just KNOW what it is. Here, too, we are obviously dealing with something ordained by nature.

When we encounter it, we experience a sense of harmony. The absolute rightness of what is beautiful. An ideal, irrevocably given us by nature, that no fashion trend could ever begin to approach.

Highly sensitive people have a heightened understanding of what is harmonious.

Leonardo da Vinci and *Michelangelo Buonarroti* are certainly prominent examples of HSPs whose understanding of harmoniousness allowed them to create astonishing works of beauty. Their gifts to humanity can never be described as "mainstream." They represent a form of perfection that people experience deep inside themselves as harmonious, as pleasing. The same is true for classical music: the music of *Beethoven, Bach,* and other *great composers* has retained its timeless appeal throughout the ages.

Although it is probably not your life goal to become one of the greatest artists or musicians in the history of mankind, you will nonetheless recognize that you, too, carry this KNOWLEDGE within you. It is the logical consequence of having an HES. You simply KNOW if something is right or wrong.

When something doesn't fit into a painting just right or when something in a piece of music sounds dissonant, only you, as an HSP, will sense this immediately. When this happens, your primal instincts have taken over. All day long, minute by minute, you will be able to sense whether everything in your surroundings is just the way it should be. In your home, on your desk, at an art exhibition, or with the smaller works of art that you have created yourself.

In your everyday work, too, you will constantly sense whether or not everything around you is harmonious. When your working environment isn't peaceful, this will make you very uncomfortable. For example, you would find it absolutely impossible to work in a large open-plan office where there is constantly a negative atmosphere. Even disputes in neighboring departments can generate a feeling of dread in you. A negative work environment can even rob you of sleep.

Some HSPs are affected by this to an extreme degree. Then, even harmless visual and tactile stimuli, smells, or sounds can actually cause them to feel so uncomfortable that they simply cannot endure this disharmonious input.

But HSPs also have a sense for the rightness of intellectual issues. When they hear about a new idea, they quickly have a definite feeling about whether or not it fits into reality. This could include work processes, corporate strategies, marketing concepts, or even simply a friend's life plans.

If the people in your private or professional circles are smart, when they need advice, they will turn to you. As long as your HES can make itself fully heard by your AES, you are even capable of acting as a sort of oracle. You will very rarely be wrong in your assessment of a situation. The company's owners would also do well to allow you to give them your feedback. If the world would pay more attention to what HSPs have to say, so many mistakes (and above all, so much lunacy) could be avoided.

Some HSPs who work as career coaches, trainers, or consultants can't always explain this ability themselves. They often then feel that they are able to predict the future. This is a fallacy, however. I don't believe that anything can be predicted. HSPs simply have a stronger sense of how things are ordered – a KNOWLEDGE of what fits harmoniously into the realm of reality. It is a form of holistic order to which every life is subject.

I'm sure I'm not telling you anything you don't already know. Perhaps you only experience your understanding of harmoniousness more indirectly. For example, it might reveal itself in your perfectly organized desktop, where everything has to be in its assigned place. Or perhaps you have an overly exaggerated sense of tidiness, which leads you to keep your home exceptionally neat, clean, and harmonious, allowing you to fulfill at least some part of your concept of what an ideal world would look like.

It could also be that you chase after only that which is beautiful (people, for instance), because this is the only thing that isn't fundamentally contradictory to your understanding of a harmonious aesthetic appearance. Or, you have suffered all your life because of your figure, since it can never measure up to your KNOWLEDGE of what a perfect body would be.

This is the downside to your understanding of what is harmonious – it can very quickly degenerate into perfectionism. And then, your gift becomes a burden. Anything that you see as being imperfect will consequently be experienced as a great affront your inner sense of harmoniousness.

At the same time, however, many HSPs are not aware that other people don't possess this same KNOWLEDGE. The people in their private and professional circles often have no idea what the term PERFECTION even entails.

If you, as an HSP, work in a managerial position, it is likely that no one ever does anything to your complete satisfaction. You then almost certainly begin to check up on everything and everybody, to be sure that every possible error is uncovered. In extreme cases, you may even decide to simply do everything yourself, since no one else can measure up to your high standards.

HSPs need to work in professions where perfection is accepted.

Cardiologists, for example, are most definitely given sufficient time and space to allow them to optimally carry out their medical duties. Here, perfectionism is called for. If, however, hospital management begins to require them to also take into account the financial aspects of their work, then the situation becomes quite different. For surgeons who are highly sensitive, this will eat away at them, and they will at some point decide that they can no longer continue to work at this particular hospital. The HSP cardiologist will probably have to open their own practice and go into business for themself.

Not everyone has this kind of option available, however. Then, the tendency toward perfectionism can actually trigger a great deal of inner conflict. If HSPs are forced to accept mistakes, to improvise on the job, or simply accept mediocre work, this can lead to absolute inner turmoil.

I have even known HSPs who couldn't sleep at night simply because a worker had hung their favorite oversized picture slightly crooked on the wall.

Your understanding of harmony and/or your tendency toward perfectionism stand in general opposition to the realities of today's working world. The universal workforce shortage and the never-ending efforts at corporate restructuring make it nearly impossible to attain optimal business operations. It is cheaper to throw a defective product onto the market than it is to slow the process down by putting it through preliminary testing and controls. It is more expedient to accept a lower level of quality than to hire more staff to allow better structures and conditions to be put in place.

Workplaces where the environment is chaotic or companies where quality is not prioritized are completely ill-suited for highly sensitive people.

2.1.2 A Strong Conscience

The conscience is another concept that is difficult to define in intellectual terms. It encompasses the HSP's heightened intuition, but it also represents a form of higher KNOWLEDGE – in this case, however, from an ethical perspective. It allows HSPs to sense more strongly than others what is morally right or wrong. Even if they haven't had the benefit of a good upbringing, they will always be able to precisely distinguish between good and evil.

As a rule, you will find it difficult to escape your conscience. It occupies a very high position in your being. Your primal instinct lets you know what is right – and, above all, what is *not* right.

HSPs have high moral and ethical values.

Your conscience is probably the only thing to which you feel duty-bound. You want to be able to act according to your own values and standards. If you were a situation where you felt compelled to trick someone, tell a white lie, or charge a customer more than was necessary, this would unquestionably cause you to lose sleep.

So, it stands to reason that you are practically fanatical when it comes to honesty. You are living in a world, however, in which the battle for market share is growing ever fiercer, practically driving companies to implement morally questionable measures. If this affects you in your role as an employee or a decision-maker, sooner or later you are likely going to feel that you have to resign.

More likely though, you will bravely hold on – usually right up until the bitter end. The reason for this is another trait that distinguishes you from non-highly sensitive people:

HSPs are loyal and want to fulfill their duty.

Your sense of duty is exceptionally strong. This makes it easy for you to be entrusted with important tasks, where no one has to check up on you to make sure that you have properly completed them. You are the essence of reliability. You KNOW what needs to be done, innately understand and follow the unspoken rules, and always punctually deliver that which you have previously promised.

Basically, you are every HR department's dream employee. You always take into consideration company resources and goals, never waste time, and consistently put customer satisfaction first. When you are allowed to work according to your own values and standards, everything runs like clockwork. No shenanigans, no tricks – simply an honest job performance.

Moreover, you are also probably capable of doing the work of two people. It is frequently only after a highly sensitive employee quits that the employer realizes that no one else can even come close to producing the same results. The next person to take the job is either overwhelmed by the complexities of the job or can't get the work done within the given timeframes. Only once the HSP is gone do many HR departments belatedly recognize the speed, precision, and effectiveness with which the work had been carried out. Now, they need additional staff, but since this is rarely approved, the entire department comes under pressure – simply because one single HSP has left.

2.1.3 Justice

Highly sensitive persons have a profound sense of justice. This, too, is a logical consequence of their extreme understanding of the harmonious – their notion of a perfect world. This

KNOWLEDGE is also hard to precisely define. Only HSPs have an unerring sense of whether a particular situation or constellation is just or not.

For example, this makes it extremely difficult for you if you hear a manager yelling at a subordinate or if other staff members go on the attack and start bullying another co-worker. It doesn't matter whether you yourself are directly affected or if you are simply an observer, your profound sense of justice will strongly inform you that something is wrong. And this will trigger a lot of anxiety.

If you are confronted with injustice in your surroundings, at work, or anywhere else in the world, this will weigh heavily on you.

HSPs want to work in a world that is just.

The figure of Robin Hood perfectly describes you – you possess a noble idealism, which is obviously very difficult to put into practice in an age in which values are no longer what matters, but rather, whether you are seen as the victor or the vanquished. You will therefore enjoy a strong sense of purpose when you have the feeling that your professional work has made the world even just a little bit more just.

2.2 INDEPENDENCE

The second major aspect that distinguishes you from non-highly sensitive people is your striving for independence. The underlying reasons for this can once again be found in your three different ego states.

You carry your closest allies within you at all times. This allows you to generally feel quite comfortable being alone, without immediate feelings of loneliness. Nearly everything you need to feel complete is already on board. You are protector (HES), achiever (AES), and helpless being (NES), all in one.

This means that when you begin to love your NES, you are actually loving yourself, and when your HES provides you with support, protection, or guidance, you are taking care of yourself. Sooner or later, you will reach a point in your PERSONAL GROWTH where you can generate love from within yourself.

Only you, as an HSP, have the innate ability to both feel love and feel loved without having to come into contact with anyone else (more on this later). You actually comprise an entire self-contained family in the form of a single person.

> Many HSPs do not generally need to rely on anyone else for their happiness.

This theory is supported by the conspicuous fact that a very high proportion of highly sensitive people find traditional family life to be extremely difficult. For HSPs, it can be a burden to have look after too many children of their own or to always have to provide those close to them with guidance and advice.

But the fact, too, that HSPs usually have very few close friends or that a conservative, traditional partnership usually pushes them to their limits is a good indicator of this secret desire to be alone. At the very least, the HSP could eventually find relationships and circumstances that are too rigid or too confining to be excessively limiting.

I will divide the topic of INDEPENDENCE into four sub-categories:

1. Freedom
2. Personal responsibility
3. Performance mindset
4. Claim to leadership

2.2.1 Freedom

Astonishingly, even the early Christians held to the belief that for their small minority, it was extremely important not to be tied down.

> *Paul's FIRST LETTER TO THE CORINTHIANS:*
>
> *"I think that in view of the present distress it is well for a person to remain as he is. Are you bound to a wife? Do not seek to be free. Are you free from a wife? Do not seek marriage. But if you marry, you do not sin, and if a girl marries she does not sin. Yet those who marry will have worldly troubles, and I would spare you that."*

But don't worry – if a partner, a family, and children are nonetheless important components of your life, this is far from a contradiction. You will, however, always be striving to maintain at least your intellectual independence.

HSPs are independent free spirits.

As you yourself KNOW, there is no such thing as true freedom. This is a sentimental term bandied about by politicians and those in the economic sector. Large corporations frequently use the concept of "freedom" to help them break into new and profitable markets. Market economies will always peddle the idea of freedom in their slogans. Only in countries with open markets can this type of advertising strategy optimally manipulate the target population – it stimulates consumer purchasing and generates the desired new corporate profits.

As a result, we merely experience a type of "freedom of consumption": the freedom to choose between different products and services. But even this freedom is limited if we don't possess sufficient financial resources. I would therefore like to restrict the definition of freedom to simply mean the absence of excessive pressure to act in a certain way.

HSPs want to perform their jobs without pressure to act in a certain way.

Your independent nature means that you want to decide for yourself what to do and when to do it. If you feel too constrained in this, it runs contrary to your desire for freedom, resulting in feelings of pressure and tension – in other words, anxiety.

The degree to which you are affected by such feelings will depend on the stage you are at in your PERSONAL GROWTH. I have interviewed HSPs who were embittered by the very fact that they were dependent on a regular salary. From their perspective, the constrictions of everyday working life were already restricting their freedom. They lived with the dream of a utopian world in which everyone was provided with sufficient resources.

It's possible that you will sense this same desire within yourself. However, you have surely also noticed a small, subtle contradiction: This longing for a universal basic income only arises in people who are still miles away from their predestined path. If they were actually working within the context of their true vocational calling, the energy they would be getting back from it would be far more than what they were investing. They would no longer think of their jobs as "work."

Nonetheless, the fact that you often wish to simply be able to kick back and just enjoy the day cannot be ignored. You want to be the master of your own time.

HSPs want to decide for themselves how to spend their time.

And so, there are many HSPs who are self-employed, including, for instance, the many freelancers who work in media, or as yoga or fitness instructors, or who are active in the fashion industry. The percentage of HSPs who work in these branches is surely very high. And there are certainly many highly sensitive professionals to be found among the innumerable freelance career coaches, trainers, and educators.

In contrast, for those employed in traditional salaried positions, the ability to set their own work schedule will be extremely important. Flextime and worktime accounts will be important options. All in all, a good compromise for HSPs would be a flexible work schedule that includes the possibility of converting accumulated overtime – whether days, weeks, or months – into time off.

Your inner desire to be able to freely and independently make decisions about your everyday work life also results in yet another personality trait.

2.2.2 Personal Responsibility

Whether you are self-employed or work for an employer, the ability to work independently will be very important to you. If your boss only wants to check in on your progress every few days or weeks, this will come very close to meeting your need for taking personal responsibility for your work.

However, the opposite will also be true: Anything that makes it obvious to you that you are not INDEPENDENT will be a source of irritation to you. This will sometimes lead you to react in a less-than-positive manner:

> You do not appreciate it when someone checks up on you or tells you how to do your job.

Even just an attempt by someone else to motivate you will not sit well with you – you will see it as restricting your INDEPENDENCE. It will make you feel pressured, even when the other person is only offering to help. You may even feel personally attacked. Their attempt to motivate you causes you to feel demeaned, which then leads you to become indignant that the other person doesn't seem to realize that you don't need their help to CONSCIENTIOUSLY deliver optimum results.

You also find it difficult to submit to the little traditions that exist in every company. These subtle internal rules are never openly discussed, but everyone abides by them. For you, though, these are just one more form of pressure to act in a certain way. Even little things like this seem like another constraint on your own personality.

All in all, if you work in a salaried position, you are going to need to have a high degree of tolerance to not feel that your INDEPENDENCE has been too constrained.

2.2.3 Performance Mindset

Most highly sensitive people prefer to impress others with their job accomplishments rather than with their personalities.

> Highly sensitive people usually prefer to be evaluated according to their achievements.

Because of their need for INDEPENDENCE, they prefer not to share too much about themselves. They would prefer that the focus remained solely on their work accomplishments. Also, HSPs hold to ideals of modesty, restraint, and a sense of duty. They KNOW how things should be done. They don't like show-offs or people who have only attained success because they are masters of self-promotion. This is why HSPs often pursue a strategy of delivering outstanding work performance rather than trying to score points with their personality.

Incidentally, most HSPs are not even aware of their desire to deliver outstanding performance at work. There are HSPs who vehemently curse the concept of meritocracy, but who consistently have a performance mindset themselves. They only respect themselves when they are able to successfully achieve their vision of a better world, and so they fanatically engage in a battle for this idealized world, satisfied only when their ideas for improving the world are taken seriously.

You've surely also felt this way at times. However, you need to be aware of the underlying cause of your over-emphasis on performance. It will likely be unpleasant to have to admit this about yourself, but:

HSPs have a strong need to be ACKNOWLEDGED.

I have deliberately used the word "acknowledged" here, rather than "respected." It is very important to distinguish between the two. What I mean is that you don't necessarily want to be "admired." Quite the contrary – you would probably even find it embarrassing if people looked up to you. You would tell yourself it was inappropriate. So, if people don't revere you, it's not a big deal to you. However, if they ignore you or treat you rudely, that IS a big deal.

At first glance, this contradicts my earlier statement that you don't need anyone else to be happy. People who are INDEPENDENT also don't usually need others to pay them any special attention. But that's not true in your case. This gives rise to another inner conflict. By the end of this book, however, this will have miraculously been resolved. Here, though, for instructive purposes, I need to focus on the isolated observation of your deep longing to be acknowledged.

In general, no one likes to be overlooked. The difference with you is that you have a distinct emotional reaction to this. These feelings play a role for you that doesn't affect non-highly sensitive people. If your colleagues or boss ignore you, forget about you, or even reject you, this can set off a dramatic reaction within you. You are in danger of interpreting this as a threat to your entire existence. This can even escalate to the point where you have thoughts of ending it all.

The underlying reason why it is almost a matter of survival for you, as an HSP, not to be ignored by the significant people in your life can once again be found in your NES. Remember: this part of your ego is comparable to a newborn and is responsible for your emotional state.

Let's take another look at what a baby is like. This endearing new little creature is at, first, fairly easy to please. It wants to sleep and be fed. And, if it is regularly cuddled and shown a bit of love, then all the better. So far, so good.

If these basic needs are not optimally met, this is, of course, extremely tragic, but it is not yet life-threatening. If a tiny infant isn't nursed on a regular schedule or if it sometimes can't sleep because it has a tummy-ache, this does not yet endanger its life. There is another situation, however, that could prove to be extremely serious:

If the baby is simply forgotten about.

If this happens, death is imminent. If a newborn is left lying somewhere unnoticed, it will soon die of hunger or cold.

Unfortunately, human newborns are not capable of surviving on their own right after birth. In comparison to some animal species, our children are born prematurely. They are not capable of getting around on their own or finding food for themselves. All they can do is lie there and hope that someone will take care of them. Human infants are therefore dependent to the utmost degree on others – otherwise they will die.

A newborn's primal instinct will always ensure that the infant makes itself noticeable. The unconscious primary task for newborns is to make sure that they will never be forgotten. That's why a newborn's instincts (when they are awake) are continually checking to see if the person who provides them with nourishment is still there or at least somewhere nearby. Babies don't have many tools at their disposal for this. They can only lie there and look around or listen. At even the tiniest suspicion, for instance, that the mother might somehow be gone, the newborn's instincts tell it that this could now be an urgent matter of life or death.

The longer that no one comes, the more intensely the battle for survival escalates.

Babies don't yet have a concept of time. They can't tell how long Mommy or Daddy needs to get from the living room to their crib. They only know the here and now. Now – at this very moment – no one is there. And, if no one is there, they know subconsciously that all is lost.

This is why, in many cultures, it is common, even today, for babies to be carried by their parents throughout the entire day. The baby is held close to the body of their caretaker and protector (mother or father) with a large wrap or something similar, to make it unmistakably clear to them at every second, without pause: *You're not going to die – I am here and will take care of you.*

To summarize, babies must therefore constantly be aware of their surroundings. If there is even the slightest hint that they might be forgotten, they must inevitably assume that death is at hand.

And now you, the HSP, enter the picture: these existential primal fears of the newborn are still affecting you today. Your NES has never stopped checking to see if anyone else is around you and who it might be. Of course, the point is no longer to make sure that someone is there to feed you – but the fears still remain.

If you notice that someone is overlooking you, or has perhaps even forgotten about you, the same feelings of danger will be awakened in you as are in the newborn who thinks it has been forgotten. The more important you consider that person to be, the more intense the feelings of fear that arise. This might include significant co-workers, people who are generally popular, or simply people in management positions. In other words, people to whom you have perhaps subconsciously attributed a parental role or whom you have trusted to provide for or protect you.

Normally, when people are ignored, they react by feeling disappointed or somewhat sad. Some people aren't bothered by it in the least. Others don't even notice that they have been overlooked. You, on the other hand, have a completely different reaction.

Your outstanding powers of observation, coupled with your strong intuition, give you the unfortunate ability to immediately sense if and in what way your presence is not being ACKNOWLEDGED by others. And then, your NES triggers precisely those feelings that would normally only arise if your survival were threatened (a tiger attack, a hurricane, a wildfire, etc.).

When HSPs feel ignored, the same stress hormones are released as would be if they were in life-threatening danger.

People who are not highly sensitive can't even begin to imagine what it does to an HSP when the customs, social norms, and universal values of human coexistence are violated.

As an HSP, if you experience unkind, rude, or inhumane behavior, a physical danger-alert system unlike any other will be triggered in you (especially if you are still at an early stage in your personal growth).

Your hormones will go into *fight-for-your-life* mode. Adrenaline, cortisol, and all the other hormones necessary for such mortal combat will be released. Only your most important organs will continue to be supplied with sufficient blood. Your blood pressure will rise, your heart rate will increase, and your muscles will be flooded with the additional oxygen and glucose they need for the looming battle.

While you are in this survival mode, your body has no time to deal with disease. Your immune system will almost completely shut down. Cancer cells, bacteria, and viruses will be able to run rampant. They will be dealt with later. Right now, your body is setting its priorities – its only focus is on sheer survival.

Stress patterns like this have their place – they can be quite useful in helping people successfully get through certain situations. For you, however, these reactions are triggered when you are just treated rudely by someone you consider important. Or if you don't receive the praise you feel you deserve, or are otherwise afraid that you won't be adequately ACKNOWLEDGED.

What makes this so dramatic is that this flood of stress hormones (triggered by the supposedly imminent battle to the death) also acts as a kind of doping. You thus have more stamina than your colleagues and can deliver an even more outstanding work performance than ever before, so that at the end of this mortal battle, you may indeed attain that which you so fervently desire.

This means that only HSPs run the risk of overlooking their body's natural physical limitations. Non-HSPs, whose bodies tire naturally, slow themselves down much sooner, but the doping effect of the stress hormones in HSPs means that they often only stop when their bodies finally collapse.

For young HSPs in particular, whose physical and psychological stress thresholds are still high, this doping effect means that they are thus capable of maintaining this inner fight for survival over the course of many years. Pumped full of stress hormones, they fail to notice that their body has long since been in emergency mode. For years, they've been running around with an almost completely non-functioning immune system. And all of this because they are afraid they won't receive sufficient recognition.

Highly sensitive people need employers, co-workers, or bosses who will appropriately ACKNOWLEDGE their achievements.

This is the only chance they have to avoid falling into an endless cycle of constantly trying to accomplish ever more so that they perhaps will finally receive the ACKNOWLEDGMENT they so urgently require.

I have observed, however, that sooner or later, nearly every highly sensitive person who works for a company will be deeply disappointed. This usually is related to a couple of specific corporate philosophies. For one, many employers are of the opinion that simply by providing a paycheck, they are showing sufficient appreciation for their employees, and for another, an increasing number of executives view their employees more as interchangeable commodities than as contributors to their operational success. This, too, is source of conflict for HSPs who work for corporate employers.

2.2.4 Claim to Leadership

Even if some of you are not yet aware of this, deep within you, there is a very dominant side of your personality. You may even be perceived as being classically egocentric. The culprit here is your NES.

Let's come back to our picture of the adorable baby: from its own subjective perspective, it is all alone in the world. At first, it doesn't have any relationship with other people (outside of its parents), nor does it have any concept of sociological comparisons. Its basic life principle is: *"I'm lying here, I'm hungry, feed me."*

A newborn baby couldn't care less whether Mommy and Daddy are at the end of their ropes or desperately just need a couple of hours of sleep. It is beyond astonishing how much tenacity these tiny little bundles of joy have in bullying their parents with their crying – a very effective management tool that gets Mommy or Daddy to spring into action whenever needed.

Deep within you, this attitude is still dormant. A part of your ego is convinced that there must be people who are supposed to spring into action for you. Your NES believes that there must indeed be helpers who will ensure that you survive.

HSP want to have people who will take care of them.

Deep down, you would rather be in charge of simply doing the thinking and having the overall responsibility.

Everything else, any task that is unpleasant, boring, or just pointless, you would generously like to delegate to others (as long as they meet your standards for perfectionism). This means that HSPs possess a kind of inner claim to leadership that is not immediately obvious to the outside world. It's a rather subtle thing. And, incidentally, very few HSPs are even aware of their dominant side. This actually means that:

HSPs feel extremely comfortable in leadership positions.

Unfortunately, this is in complete contradiction to the more reserved nature of HSPs, and many of them therefore limit themselves to acting this out on a more subtle level. We then see spouses or bosses who are being indirectly managed. They are led to believe that they are holding the reins, but they have actually long since been fulfilling the wishes of the HSP.

2.3 CREATIVE POWERS

Along with your intuitive KNOWLEDGE and your enormous striving for INDEPENDENCE, there is another personality trait that strongly sets you apart from others: your impressive CREATIVE POWERS.

I sub-divide this trait into the following three aspects:

1. Intuition
2. Creativity
3. Inventiveness

2.3.1 Intuition

As you've already learned, your intuitive abilities are your greatest highly sensitive gift. They are the result of your extremely powerful HIGHER EGO STATE. This ego state serves as a quite useful internal and external guide. Or, to put it a bit more sentimentally:

> Your INTUITION can be thought of as a kind of internal guardian angel.

Many HSPs have a certain conviction that there is something deep within them that ultimately has their best interests at heart, but they don't trust themselves enough to actually rely on this. And they're not wrong about this. After all, you have to have gained some life experience to understand how your INTUITION actually functions in your everyday life.

Not only is the functioning of your INTUITION imperceptible to your senses, but it also works most effectively when you are NOT relying on it.

As you also already know, a certain portion of your ego consists of a fearful and fragile NES. Until you have fully taken care of its needs, it will not be possible for your AES (in other words, you, yourself) to tap into the full potential of your INTUITION. Only once your NES feels safe and secure will you be able to take advantage of the great power of your intuitive abilities. There is a specific reason for this:

Fear sabotages your intuitive abilities.

This means that there is actually a list of priorities for your life. You first have to satisfy your NES's need for protection and security before you can even begin to experience any of life's happy coincidences. Incidentally, I am going to go into this in great detail in Chapter 3.

Basically, your INTUITION operates on an unconscious level. You're not going to hear any voices telling you what to do (and if you do, please seek medical or psychological help immediately!) You also aren't going to be able to tap into your HES through meditation any other such intellectual approaches. Unfortunately, you will never be able to discern intellectually whether your mind is playing tricks on you or your HES is at work. Consequently, your ordinary senses are only going to be able to perceive your intuitive powers as external manifestations – events in your surroundings – which will usually consist of coincidences, strokes of luck, or happy quirks of fate.

It will usually only become clear to you in hindsight that you have once again taken the right path or had a sixth sense about something. You can ruminate on this until your brain is white-hot (take another look at the cover of this book), but you will never be able to consciously or cognitively experience your INTUITION.

What this means is that it is actually only your mind. – i.e., your AES – that can throw a wrench in the works. It is simply the nature of things that your conscious mind wants to plan, understand, and control. However, this is completely contradictory to living an INTUITIVELY LED LIFE.

The more that HSPs want to have control over their lives, the less they can reap the advantages of their intuitive powers.

It is only human nature to want to control our lives. But let's not fool ourselves: this need for control is always rooted in fear – and it is exactly this fear that sabotages our intuitive gifts. This is precisely the decisive crux of the problem. The more that HSPs stubbornly hold onto specific concepts or ideas about how they should live their lives, the greater the danger that they will go down the wrong paths, experience upheaval, and suffer disappointments. An excessive, urgent need for control can even end tragically in a basic repudiation of life.

For those who are interested in the scientific aspects of intuition, I recommend the essays and studies of *Henning Plessner*, a psychologist from Heidelberg, Germany, as well as those of the psychologist *Gerd Gigerenzer* (director of the Max Planck Institute for Human Development). Both of these psychologists have been able to demonstrate, in a valid and precise way, that the decisions we make intuitively have a much higher success rate than do those we make on a purely intellectual basis.

Off in the distance, I noticed a cat. It suddenly froze – it had spotted some birds in a nearby tree. You could see its instincts take over as it crouched at the edge of a building and waited, never taking its eyes off the tree.

I expected it to attack immediately, but it did absolutely nothing at first. In fact, it almost appeared that the cat was simply bored. It just sat there, without moving. I slowly became impatient. "Is something going to happen or not?" I wondered. I eventually lost track of the situation, turning my attention back to the newspaper I had been reading on my terrace. Several minutes must have gone by.

Then, out of the corner of my eye, I suddenly noticed that something was indeed happening. The cat still sat in the exact same position as before. "It's certainly patient," I thought to myself, "Very impressive, little kitty, but the birds are still sitting there in the tree. You're going to have to make a move." At that very moment, a little finch flew toward the cat and landed right under its nose. With a single blow, the little bird's tragic fate was sealed.

"Poor little bird," I thought, "but how could you be so stupid as to land right in front of the cat's nose?"

How had the cat managed to do this? Did it somehow know that at some point its prey would land right there?

This little anecdote is a perfect example of the difference between conscious thought and instinct (intuition). Animals have little if any consciousness (depending on their evolutionary stage). They act and react on an almost exclusively unconscious level. They are still completely guided by their instincts.

Now, I assume that you have no desire to stalk innocent little birds. Still, you are equipped with the same instinct for hunting. At some point, you won't be thinking about anything in particular, and suddenly, exactly what you had been wishing for will appear right in front of you. This powerful gift is possibly the greatest difference between you and non-highly sensitive people.

Your INTUITION is therefore capable of establishing exactly the right conditions for your highly sensitive life. As if guided by some magical powers, you will meet the right people, be in the right place, or experience other highly significant existential co-incidences. It's important to note here, that your INTUITION doesn't actually change your circumstances (or anything else in the world), but simply guides you to surroundings that are better suited to your interests. Assuming, of course, that you trust in it and are fully participating in life.

Basically, all living things are interconnected by way of the INVISIBLE WORLD (or the quantum level) – which, incidentally, is no longer even disputed in the scientific world (for one example of this, see the *Hong-Ou-Mandel experiment involving twin photons* conducted by the British-American physicist *Leonard Mandel*).

This is comparable to your home computer, which, theoretically, can connect via the internet to every other computer on earth. In the same way, your HES is also capable of connecting with the HES of other people. Think of it as a kind of mental World Wide Web.

In a practical sense, your HES functions in the same way as your Wi-Fi router. Just as the router helps your computer to connect to the internet, your HES allows you to connect to a world that cannot be seen. Its function is like that of your Wi-Fi, which is always active in the background, and whose connection to the internet continuously provides your smart phone or computer with massive amounts of data. You, however, only see the limited results that appear on your screen.

This explains why highly sensitive people typically have the ability to immediately and correctly assess people or surroundings. HSPs enter a room and immediately sense what is going on. Or you meet someone for the first time and quickly form an opinion about that person's state of mind or their intentions. In cases like this, your HES has connected to the other person's HES via a world that you cannot perceive with your senses. You are receiving information from the other person, which then diffusely makes its way into the conscious portion of your brain. This means that your independently operating HES is continuously receiving information about your surroundings and transmitting this information to your AES. This is why you can always rely on what HSPs say when they are assessing the influences at work in what is happening around them.

HSPs are generally able to accurately assess their surroundings.

Of course, there will be times when you wish you didn't have to perceive certain things. Still, I can assure you that the advantages of having such finely tuned antennae far outweigh the disadvantages. You can put your INTUITION to effective use not only in your private life, but, most especially, in your professional life.

HSPs have a sixth sense for what works and what doesn't.

Actually, this is a trait shared by only the most successful entrepreneurs. HSPs therefore possess a talent that allows them to develop a profitable sense for business.

It's also conceivable, however, that you are currently working for an employer. In that case, you will surely frequently find yourself in situations where you have to carry out certain corporate strategies that you KNOW are absolutely ridiculous. In these situations, you will feel a deep sense of futility. While your co-workers don't give it a second thought and simply blindly follow management's instructions, you will constantly have to battle inner conflicts.

The same is true when your INTUITION tells you that your boss is lying to you or if you are forced to work in a team where most of its members are frustrated co-workers. In each of these cases, you will surely wish that you didn't have to perceive everything that is going on. Still, I repeat: With your INTUITION, you have an extremely powerful tool in your hands.

It's highly probable that you have often narrowly avoided some mishap or another without even having been aware of this. You can never know for sure how often your INTUITION has jumped in at the last second or had already sprung in action to protect you from unpleasant situations.

2.3.2 Creativity

You are undoubtedly a very creative person. This is a pleasant by-product of your strong connection to the INVISIBLE WORLD.

Creativity is nothing more than a connection to the realm of ideas. Christians call this realm the *Holy Spirit*, in the esoteric world, this is referred to as the *Akasha Chronicles*, and physicists speak of *dark energy* or the *quantum level*. It has been acknowledged by virtually every philosopher that new ideas don't simply spring from our minds, but only arrive there or are received there.

Even the elite among the astrophysicists have come to agree that 95% of our world is made up of a medium that is not only imperceptible to our senses, but which has a determining influence over our lives (for an example of this, see the *Millennium Run* simulations of dark matter conducted at the *Max Planck Institute for Astrophysics, in Garching, Germany).*

For instance, as I am writing these words, I am basically not thinking about anything at all. I am using my AES only to write down what I am receiving. In other words, I am essentially only acting as a secretary for my HES. You are therefore reading a book whose contents were not only acquired but also written down by my intuitive abilities.

All creative people not only know such situations too well but are also consciously able to create the conditions favorable for it. They don't spend their time brooding over or trying to figure out the pros and cons. They simply patiently wait for the moment when they will be touched by the muse. When they are finally in this creative flow, everything seems to happen automatically. The channel is open and the ideas (words, designs, colors, shapes, etc.) literally spill out.

If you haven't yet experienced this fantastic feeling, then it is high time that you did. It's not limited to just the fine arts, nor does it always have to be about singing, acting, or making music. It may be that you are talented in one of these art forms, but your creative bandwidth is much greater than just these. Basically, every idea you have in your everyday life is a part of your CREATIVITY. Everything that you come up with no instruction or prior knowledge, and which hasn't been borrowed from someone else, belongs to this category.

The creativity that HSPs possess isn't limited to the arts but comprises the entire bandwidth of ideas they have in both their private and professional lives.

Actually, being able to read music or follow a script doesn't really count as a true act of creativity. CREATIVITY involves the actual composition of a piece of music or the authoring of a screenplay. Everything that you bring into reality from the INVISIBLE WORLD, making it visible, audible, smellable, or palpable to those who are not highly sensitive, falls precisely under the definition of CREATIVITY (see Chapter 1, "Putting it All Together: *Highly sensitive people are intermediaries between the visible and the invisible world*).

Even just coping with a difficult life situation requires a lot of CREATIVITY. If serious financial, familial, or professional problems arise, it takes a lot of creative thinking just to somehow satisfactorily get through the day. But such things as the start-up of a manufacturing plant in a distant foreign country can also call for an enormous amount of CREATIVITY. If a technician who works there doesn't come up with the right idea at the right time, it is going to make the task incredibly difficult to accomplish.

It's therefore important to realize that your creative talents may not necessarily lie in playing an instrument or being a singer or painter. Your creativity actually goes much deeper than this. It enables you to come up with ideas that allow something completely new to emerge, whether on a large or a small scale. And this brings us to yet another highly sensitive gift that could prove to be very lucrative in your professional life.

2.3.3 Inventiveness

In my opinion, the majority of all great inventions are the work of a highly sensitive person. This includes, of course, all of the researchers, scientists, and engineers who have accomplished great things. However, all of the philosophers and spiritual leaders who have provided the world with so much wisdom may also have been highly sensitive.

Perhaps it is now clear to you why you seem to be constantly seeking. Those who seek also desire to find. This trait is deeply rooted within you:

HSPs have a desire to find something.

This means that you are always searching for something new. Your entire life, you've probably had the feeling of not being satisfied with what you had. A little like the saying: *Perfect is the enemy of good.*

Though you may have had several intimate relationships or affairs, held a number of different jobs, completed innumerable training sessions and continuing education courses, or maybe even traveled the world, you have probably never been truly satisfied. Every time you thought you were finally doing the right thing, after a while, it always turned out not to be the case. Either you became bored with the whole situation or it turned out to be different than what you had imagined. All of this is connected to your fantastic spirit of INVENTIVENESS, that is, your desire to be creative.

HSPs are always seeking improvement.

In a way, it's as though you are on a quest for the holy grail. You are, in the broadest sense, an inventor, and an inventor can only invent that which doesn't already exist. This could include words of wisdom, products, services, or even concepts that no one has ever thought of before. And, if you have a job where you are continually assigned new projects, your proclivity for creating something new will really serve you well. Even if you were – or are – self-employed, the task of coming up with new marketing strategies or business concepts will actually be something you really enjoy (as long as you have enough people to help out with the more mundane tasks).

2.4 PUTTING IT ALL TOGETHER

Take another look at the skills, talents, and gifts that HSPs possess and let them sink in:

1. You possess KNOWLEDGE that others do not have.
2. You cherish INDEPENDENCE.
3. You are a CREATOR of new things.

You are therefore not a run-of-the-mill employee who simply does what the boss tells them to do. You are something else entirely:

HSPs are innovators.

Over the course of this book, I will discuss in more detail exactly what it is that you actually want to INVENT.

At this point in the book, however, something quite different must have already occurred to you:

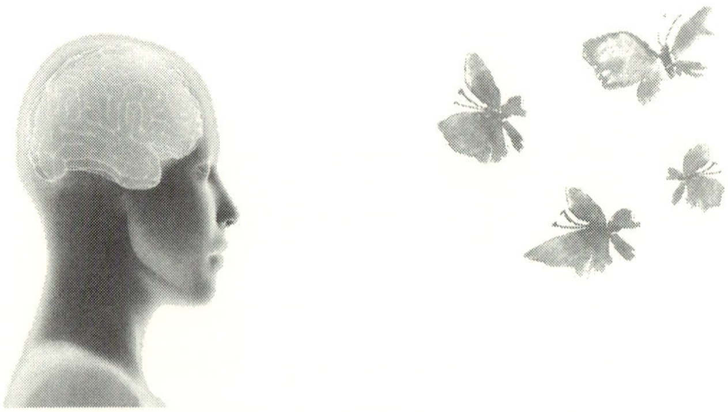

You are not a typical employee.
Secretly, you would like to be the employer.

If you had a job as a production worker on an assembly line, you would have to find things to do in your free time that would compensate for this and keep you from shriveling up inside. Even if you work in an office, though, if your job consists of only administrative duties or carrying out tasks, sooner or later, you are going to hate your job. You want to be independent, creative, and innovative.

This is why, when you are job-hunting, for you, it is less about the specific job description and more about the working conditions. You want to be able to work in a certain way. You will only be able to be happy as an employee if your workplace gives you the opportunity to work independently and creatively to INVENT something new. Such positions do, of course, exist, but with every year that goes by, they become more rare. The reason for this lies in the changes that have taken place in the labor market.

Today, employees are reminded more and more frequently that they are just cogs in the corporate wheel and are simply to do as they are told. Out-of-control market mechanisms are driving an increasing number of companies into an existential battle for survival. This has led to harsher, less-friendly working environments.

Company owners put pressure on managers and board members, which they then pass on to the people who work for them, and eventually, this all trickles down to the employee level. The pressure on the staff increases. In many companies, all of this leads to a toxic environment. HSPs find fewer and fewer opportunities to fulfill their needs for contributing new IDEAS, being ACKNOWLEDGED, or participating in INNOVATION.

Perhaps you are one of those who has already realized this and has already become self-employed. If so, the increasingly stiff competition is going to require you to know precisely what you are doing.

There is, however, a ray of hope: as an HSP, you are one of the rare people who have a strong HES. This gives you the potential to smoothly maneuver through all kinds of difficulties. All you have to do is simply ensure that your INTUITION is actually functioning, because regardless of the type of system you are living under or what the conditions there are:

Your INTUITION will always guide you to a niche where you feel comfortable.

So, before you set off on the search for your true vocational calling, there is one more minor (or perhaps, in fact, major) challenge for you to conquer: first, you have to awaken your INTUITION – your HES – from its slumber. To do this, it may mean LETTING GO of some of your preconceived ideas.

3 What Do I Need to Do to Let Go?

To repeat: Your HES can only function at full power when your life is as carefree as possible. Since cares and worries are actually a form of fear, however, your NES is once again the center of focus in this chapter:

> Not until your NES's needs are satisfied can the true power of your INTUITION fully unfold.

This means that you must first LET GO of any preconceptions you may have about your life that are unrelated to the needs of your NES. This sounds completely absurd at first, but, as previously mentioned, you have to satisfy the needs of your NES before any progress can be made. Your AES's conscious thoughts are only there to help you accept the wishes of your NES and, above all, to successfully put these into action.

This is usually the biggest misunderstanding HSPs run into – especially in the first half of their lives. They fail to recognize the inner needs of the NEWBORN EGO STATE. Instead, the ADULT EGO STATE takes over and comes up with its own ideas of how life is to be led. These ideas, however, are largely inspired by our parents, others around us, the media, or sometimes simply by marketing experts. These outside influences kindle perceived needs that don't align with the true needs of your NES. It's as though an alien being has taken over your thinking.

The first order of business, therefore, is to check to see if, indeed, you may be living your life according to ideas and concepts that haven't originated within you, yourself, but which you have simply adopted from the outside. Before you can minimize any external influences, you are first going to have recognize them. You are going to have to let go of misconceptions about how you should live your life. Any friendly spirits you may have called upon for guidance need to be sent right back where they came from. This is going to take a certain degree of courage on your part – a unique form of bravery is called for here:

To accept the present, you will need to exercise a great deal of humility.

This process will help give you more clarity about yourself and the world around you. The lightbulbs will begin to go off – and you will begin to stand with both feet planted ever more firmly on the ground.

Doing things in this order – making sure that your NES is taken care of first before turning your attention to yourself (meaning your AES) – is another paradox of your highly sensitive personality. Unfortunately, though, there is no way around it. You must first turn your attention to this seemingly secondary part of your ego before everything else can be happily resolved.

I don't want to give you any false hope, however. There are HSPs who have wandered off the path for so long in their private lives or in their professions that they will likely need the same amount of time to get back on course. They now have to DISentangle themselves from innumerable ENtanglements, as it were. You have to free yourself from any shackles you may have placed upon yourself in the past.

The speed with which you will discover your vocational calling depends on how far you have strayed from your life path so far.

At this point, I would like to ask the indulgence of those readers who may currently be caught up in extreme ENTANGLEMENTS. In what follows, I am sure that some of the recommendations I am about to make will seem completely outlandish, especially from their perspective. They may well think: *It's easy for him to talk! If he only knew ...*

But there is also another target group, who, in contrast, must only undertake a few minor changes in their lives to be able to once again fully access their powers of INTUITION. My desire is to address all of my readers, regardless of where they may find themselves on the personal growth spectrum. So, if any of my suggestions are not applicable or feasible in your current situation, at least you will know where the journey is leading. Whatever you do, however, don't put any pressure on yourself – this is also counter-productive to being able to access your HES. Any added pressure to act would be harmful (more on this later):

You don't need to do anything immediately!

And above all, you don't have to do anything perfectly. It's time to start LETTING GO of your tendency to be a perfectionist (this is the one thing you *are* allowed to do immediately). Some HSPs are so performance-driven in even their attempts to *relax* that even this becomes overwhelming. This leads to an additional stress on their nervous system, inevitably triggering in*flam*mation in their bodies. Any in*flam*mation is a sign that there is an overload of electricity in the nervous system (electrical impulses produced in the brain). This negative nervous condition is also referred to as *cerebralization* or *intellectualization.* If you are experiencing in*flam*mation of the skin, joints, or digestive system, it is therefore high time to begin LETTING GO. If certain symptoms of nervous overload are already present in the region of your head itself (e.g., migraines, eye infections, tinnitus, sinus infections, etc.), then this is really a sign that your body is on *red alert.*

And this brings us to the main topic: LETTING GO means nothing more than simply minimizing unnecessary thought processes in our brains – protecting your AES (your intellect) and putting out the *flames* in your brain.

In the esoteric community, there is even a fitting description of the process of LETTING GO:

You have to ground yourself.

Psychologists speak in terms of being in touch with reality, being centered, or concentrating on the present moment. In other words, you have to make your peace with reality.

Only fully grounded people should follow their intuition.

You can think of BECOMING GROUNDED in terms of taking the first step toward establishing a direct connection to the perceptible world (reality) through your normal senses. At this point in the book, we are therefore *not* dealing with the INVISIBLE WORLD, but with the VISIBLE WORLD. In this first step, the primary focus is not on your thoughts, but, more importantly, on your emotions.

Only by feeling can you only ease the load on your brain.

In contrast to thoughts, which generate electrical impulses in your brain and therefore tend to correspond to the principle of electricity, feelings are more appropriately categorized under the principle of magnetism. For example, if you were to hold an industrial-strength magnet to your head, you would indeed experience feelings, but these would be of an artificially induced, technical nature. At that moment, it would feel as though you were having some sort of spiritual experience. This is proof that feelings are nothing more than magnetic processes in our bodies *(for more information, see, e.g., the magnetic simulations conducted by the late Dr. Michael Persinger, Laurentian University, Ontario, Canada)*.

So, if your thoughts (electricity) are paired with certain related feelings (magnetism), then it follows logically that a type of electromagnetism will be generated. This is, as it were, the medium that connects you to the earth. You might say that you develop a "feel" for the present moment. This means that when you experience a feeling about your present surroundings, you are, in practical terms, GROUNDED. You are living in the here and now. You perceive the present moment not only cognitively, but emotionally. Your brain's thought and processing mechanisms meet up with freely flowing emotions. There are no electrical or magnetic conflicts – all is well. Your body is functioning just as nature intended it to.

Now, however, we have to deal the challenge posed by the fact that you don't yet have an ordinary inner child, but only a highly fragile NEWBORN EGO STATE. And precisely this fragile part of your ego holds ultimate responsibility for your exceedingly important emotional realm. So, you need to determine your NEWBORN EGO STATE's emotional status.

HSPs need to check in with themselves to see if they can still sense an emotion tied to every situation they find themselves in.

It is more than likely that your NES is not capable of this. And there's a good reason for this: your NES is generally quite fearful. And this means it is capable of only two different emotional states: *being afraid* and *not being afraid.* Any other emotions or emotional nuances may have been lost. Normal emotions – those which a non-HSP experiences – can no longer be generated. But because no one on earth could survive without those normal everyday emotions, the HSP's ADULT EGO STATE is forced to reactivate the need for feelings from its memory. This means that everything in their environment is linked to emotions they have already experienced in the past. We then see HSPs who consider themselves to be highly emotional, but who are no longer aware that the emotions they are triggering for any and everything have nothing to do with the actual moment at hand. At this point, everything – not only thoughts, but feelings – has been taken over by the ADULT EGO STATE. Since nature never intended this part of our ego to perform this task, it is inevitable that it will run up against the limits of its capabilities. This unhealthy intellectual process is also referred to as *interpretation.* Every picture, every statement, every person, and every day-to-day situation is interpreted through emotional experiences from the past. This results in highly emotional reactions, in which, however, not a single new feeling has actually been generated. The ego of the HSP in question now consists only of an AES, which has had to take over the work of the inactive inner child.

A person whose emotions are fed only by memories of the past or projections of the future cannot be said to be truly living. The opposite of living, however, is to be dead. And all of this is the result of a NEWBORN EGO STATE that no longer dares to experience any emotions because it is constantly tormented by PRIMAL FEARS.

It is widely acknowledged, however, that fears play an important protective role for our survival. They heighten our sensitivity to danger and enhance (for a limited period of time) our physical capabilities (e.g., through the release of stress hormones). This allows us to better defend ourselves in dangerous situations.

If you were to talk to a psychotherapist, this is what you would be told: *Today, most of these primal fears are unfounded. They stem from a time when we were still dressed in loincloths, hunting woodly mammoths. In our civilized world, these genetic relics no longer serve a purpose.*

As you might imagine, statements like these are not very satisfying to highly sensitive people. For them, it is obvious that there is indeed a very concrete reason why some fears may still serve a purpose. The protective function of these fears is something that HSPs need, especially during the first half of their lives.

As I have explained at length, in our "civilized" society, you aren't likely to be openly physically assaulted (which is punishable) – the assault will be much more subtle, and it will be on an emotional (non-punishable) level. Humankind's inner beast is as vicious as ever.

While non-HSPs are slow to recognize psychological attacks (and often aren't aware of them at all), this is, unfortunately, not true for you as an HSP. Your antennae are highly tuned to this uniquely insidious form of assault. For you, psychological attacks can cause even deeper wounds than physical violence.

It goes without saying, of course, that this can be taken too far. Understanding that your fears are a kind of early warning system is a good thing. Being plagued by them your entire life, however, is *not.* What's more, it is absolutely imperative that you let go of any exaggerated fears so that you will finally be able to tap in the intuitive powers of your HES. You should therefore not only increase your emotional resilience through specialized training (*confrontation therapy, desensitization training, exercises for overcoming fears and anxieties, etc.*) but you should also improve certain basic aspects of your life to help preclude these fears from arising in the first place.

You must first safeguard your NEWBORN EGO STATE.

The first step in the process of LETTING GO is to simply become aware of your fears so that you can begin to deal with them. It will take until the final step for your fears to ultimately be dissolved. That means that for right now, the priority is on providing your NES with at least a minimum degree of security, peace of mind, and protection.

I am aware that for the majority of HSPs, this is precisely the reason they are searching for their vocational calling. Their expectation is that if they find the right vocation, this will provide them with security and peace of mind. In addition, many HSPs also believe that this will solve all of their problems at once, since they expect their vocation to provide them with a greater sense of purpose and more enjoyment of life. I must tell you, though, that things rarely happen in this order.

Unfortunately, you can't put the second step before the first. You must *first* create more peace of mind in your life – or, in other words, you must *first* overcome your NES's fears. Only then can your true intuition function properly and lead you directly to your vocational calling.

If you don't adhere to this sequence, you may find yourself in an agonizing never-ending Catch-22:

1. Having too many worries interferes with being able to access your intuition – and this is the very thing you need to help you discover your vocational calling.

2. Until you discover your vocational calling, you will continue to have even more worries.

3. Additional worries will reduce your intuitive abilities even more, pushing the discovery of your vocational calling further and further off into the future.

4. etc., etc., etc.

I can assure you that, for years, I also tried putting the second step before the first. I was stuck in a vicious cycle – until the moment I finally began to see the light and could LET GO of many of my (externally influenced) preconceived ideas. I know this all sounds quite paradoxical. However, virtually every HSP who has found their vocational calling will confirm that it only works in this order.

To summarize, your NES plays the leading role in this chapter. You must help it attain a state of calmness so that your true intuition can emerge. The following aspects will be key in this process:

1. Taking Breaks
2. External Stimuli
3. The Mainstream
4. Your Income
5. Your Attitude Toward Your Job
6. Self-Centeredness
7. Self-Promotion
8. Sources of Stress

AUTHOR'S NOTE

I would like to remind you again at this point that all of the advice in this chapter is intended only for a temporary phase of your life. In other words, it is not meant to apply to your entire highly sensitive existence – after all, you can't spend your entire life LETTING GO. The point is to be able to get back to your natural, primal flow of life within a specific period of time. Once this has been accomplished, or once you have found your vocational calling, different life principles will normally be in force than those in the LETTING GO phase.

3.1 TAKING BREAKS

As an HSP, your sleep rhythm is very distinctly different from that of non-HSPs. The reason for this lies once again with your NES. If you take a closer look at how babies behave in the period right after they are born, your own preferred sleeping and eating rhythms will become more understandable.

To refresh your memory: Newborn babies do nothing more at first than to sleep, eat, and clamor for their caretakers. During their initial time on this earth, this is essentially all these loveable little creatures need.

Babies thereby expect to be fed every couple of hours. Around the clock. And this expectation from your earliest days still has an influence on you. In contrast to others, you seem to need to fit in more moments during the day for a little a bite to eat. This also explains your desire to take daytime naps. If you constantly find yourself feeling tired in the middle of the day, this is nothing to be concerned about. You just have an existential need to sleep more frequently than do non-highly sensitive people.

Let's take a look at your eating habits: It's likely that you need your blood sugar level to be higher – or at least more stable – than other people's. The same applies to your need to stay hydrated. Many HSPs prefer to eat more – and, above all, more regularly and frequently – than do others, and to drink a lot of water.

Eating small but frequent meals can significantly improve an HSP's mental state. Considering the higher activity level and degree of intensity in their (red-hot) brains, it is only logical that they will require fairly sophisticated nutrition and hydration strategies.

It's also therefore understandable that many HSPs become uncomfortable if they don't eat or drink something every few hours. I myself find that I just need a couple of bites of food and a large glass of water to help ward off any oncoming vague feelings of irritability (which disturbs my concentration). I have learned that for me personally, there is often no underlying reason for my moodiness – it is simply the result of my blood sugar level being too low.

Be sure to take plenty of breaks to eat and drink something.

You may struggle with being overweight, however. Most HSPs resolve this by eliminating the usual three large meals per day and instead eating more frequently, but in smaller amounts.

The occasional splurge is also an important part of enjoying life, though, and HSPs do, of course, indulge themselves to culinary treats. Just not three times a day.

The danger remains that eating will nonetheless become an overly important source of pleasure and you'll end up using food to reward yourself. This can definitely turn into an addiction. Many HSPs are aware that tasty foods (chocolate, for instance) are very effective at quickly improving their mood. Lots of them spend the entire day thinking about what sort of fabulous meal they will prepare for themselves that evening. Especially those long-suffering employees whose jobs revolve around performing mundane tasks will begin to realize that the only things that really bring them pleasure are eating and drinking. And, of course, this includes everything else you can shove into your mouth. Cigarettes, alcohol, and other drugs are also part of this category. In this instance, too, of course, feelings can be generated that have not been triggered by any actual event (more on this later).

Let's turn now to our actual topic: Many HSPs state that they can get by on only a very few hours of sleep, but that they then need to sleep more frequently.

Once again, you can see the rhythm of the newborn at work. HSPs who work in creative fields, in particular, often report that they only need four to five hours of sleep at night, but that they then nap during the day. This may be especially conducive to their creative thinking – and there is a reason for this as well:

Your HES is still active, even while you are sleeping.

A perfect example of this can be seen in the most famous inventor of all time – *Thomas Edison*. He was even known to sleep on top of the desk in his office. His best ideas always came to him just as he was waking from one of his many naps (which he spread out throughout the day). When he awoke, he was already in his work environment, thus minimizing the danger he would forget his ideas. He could immediately commit his inspirations to paper. I, too, begin to write as soon as I wake up. The information and inspiration my HES has provided me with as I slept are still fully accessible in my memory. This pleasant flow of ideas also works just as well as I awake from my treasured afternoon nap (when I get the chance to take one).

The intuitive guidance that comes to us as we sleep provides a strong sense of security. Over time, we not only become absolutely certain that our HES exists, but we realize that it is always there, providing us with fantastic new ideas.

Make note of what comes to mind
as you are waking up.

When you are dealing with a problem, make it a habit, if at all possible, to put off trying to resolve it until the next day. You need to sleep on it overnight. And then, don't make the mistake of getting right to work the minute you get up. You need at least 30 minutes of absolute calm after waking up to allow the information you have received as you were sleeping to come into your conscious mind. Otherwise, you are cutting yourself off from a valuable source of ideas. It may be that your HES has been trying for years to give you some important information in the morning, but that you've never noticed.

Incidentally, this marvelous phenomenon has a very simple explanation. While it is true, of course, that your body needs sleep in order to relax and recuperate, this does not apply equally to your mind. During the time you are sleeping, your brain is maximally active – this is in no way a time of relaxation. While you sleep, a veritable fireworks display is taking place between your ears.

As I already indicated at the beginning of this book, this is the data exchange taking place between you and the INVISIBLE WORLD. All of the information your brain has taken in throughout the day will be "uploaded" (your intuitive Wi-Fi) and, in return, your brain will receive new sets of data, providing you with many important updates for your thinking, ideas, and insights. From this perspective, your brain is actually both the transmitter and the receiver of information. It is no longer the sole location from which all of your bodily functions are initiated or influenced (which is still the assumption in the medical profession, as they don't wish to acknowledge the scientific findings from quantum physics).

Basically, what is happening here, once again, are electrical and magnetic processes. At the end of the day, your entire brain is nothing more than a generator of electromagnetic energy. And because your brain basically transforms all stimuli into images, sounds, and feelings, this activity also applies while you are sleeping. This makes it easy to understand why, during the data exchange between you and the INVISIBLE WORLD, concrete ideas emerge – they are sort of a "side effect." We refer to this process as "dreaming" (another topic that still confounds the medical profession).

This also makes clear why babies have to sleep so much at first. In a figurative sense, you can compare this process to what happens when you buy a brand-new computer or want to set up your new smart phone. If you want to get your new device up and running at top performance, there are a few things you have to take care of first. You have to configure your preferences, install apps, download software from the internet, set up a fire wall, etc., etc., etc.

It takes a little time to get your device working the way you want it to. Once you have it set up, though, you can work with it for a long time without having to constantly make changes. The basic configuration has been established. This process is similar to what happens in the computer (brain) of a newborn as well.

For the body to prepare itself for life, an enormous amount of data must be exchanged. Virtually all of the synapses in the brain must still be (correctly) linked and the body has to become physically equipped to handle any challenge that comes its way. At the beginning of a new life, there is simply a lot to be done.

I know that this comparison with a newly acquired electronic device is quite impersonal (I ask all new parents to forgive me), but I believe that the model of a human being who has just come into the world is a fitting metaphor to help us understand the brain activity that takes place while we are sleeping.

Since, as an HSP, you possess an extremely strong HES, it only makes sense that, even as an adult, these processes are still taking place within you at their highest level. It could be that the only reason you haven't yet found the right path is because your current job has forced you to suppress your natural sleep rhythm.

> You will be able to regulate your
> entire life while you sleep.

This is another example of the typical sort of conflict that exists in a traditional employer-employee relationship. The modalities of today's working world make it very difficult for HSPs to establish an optimal sleep cycle. The Spanish custom from earlier times of breaking up the workday with an extended siesta would be just about perfect for you. Likewise, so would being the manager of a small shop that stayed closed for lunch until 4pm, letting you get in your afternoon nap.

Helen could never sleep for more than five hours at a time. This meant, though, that she would get extremely tired every four to six hours. As an HSP, she realized early on that she would have to re-structure her working life accordingly.

So, right after work, she would lie down for a nap, and usually wake up again two hours later. She was then wide awake and could enjoy the evening and her leisure-time activities. Of course, this also meant that she wouldn't be tired again until very late in the evening, so it became her habit to go to bed around 1:00am.

She took advantage of the flextime option at her job to be able to go to work when she woke up on her own again, which was usually between 6:00 and 7:00am. Because she knew she would be tired again by lunch time, she taught herself an autosuggestion technique. This allowed her to completely tune out the world as she took a walk in a near-by park, and left her feeling refreshed.

In combination with consuming plenty of water and protein bars over the course of the day, she was able to strike a good compromise between her eating and sleeping needs and the demands of her job.

If you are forced work long hours with no opportunity to get away periodically, you should at least build a few intervals into your day where you can enter a sleep-like state. To be able to do this, it would be helpful to learn a relaxation technique – many autosuggestion and meditation techniques are especially well-suited for this. These will never completely make up for a lack of sleep, but they are far better than simply accepting the permanent strain on your brain.

You can use relaxation techniques to compensate for a lack of sleep.

Meditation in particular, however, carries with it a slight risk. You must be sure to use only certain specific techniques. Those that are appropriate for you include any methods that involve focusing on something specific or imagining something concrete. The only way to prevent overloading your brain (cerebralization) is to avoid losing yourself in nothingness on some distant planet.

This last bit of advice is critical for you. Your brain is already burning red-hot – you don't need to put any more demands on it. If you use the wrong meditation technique, it could lead to further strain on your brain. This would then result in you not being able to sleep at all. You would bring about the exact opposite of what you had intended to do, which could potentially cause you to feel disoriented and more anxious than before.

Before you start a meditation program, be sure to research it thoroughly.

To summarize, it can definitively be said that it is existentially important for you to take numerous breaks to eat and sleep. If your job prevents you from taking an afternoon nap or if relaxation techniques don't seem to work for you, you should at least try to find another way to give your mind a break.

At the very least, use your lunch break to distract yourself from work.

Getting out for a walk in natural surroundings or even just enjoying a cup of coffee somewhere out in the fresh air would be great examples of this. You absolutely need to take breaks from work and these need to be times when you are not thinking about your job. It wouldn't make any sense, for instance, to spend your break time discussing work-related issues with a colleague. Still, a lot of people feel uncomfortable spending their breaks alone. They are afraid they will become excluded from the group dynamic. After all, the company cafeteria is also a place where people can promote their careers and gather insider information.

Unfortunately, I can't offer you a perfect solution for this. I can only say this much: If you fail to take enough breaks from your work, sooner or later your performance will suffer. This will be more damaging to your career than not hanging around for a half an hour during the lunch break.

In summary, sleep (or at least, rest) is perhaps the most powerful tool you have at your disposal. Through it, you will receive all the information that is critical for your life and for finding your vocational calling. Sleep can generate so much of what is fundamentally essential to your highly sensitive being. More on this later.

3.2 EXTERNAL STIMULI

At the beginning of this book, I described what life was like for you in your mother's womb. You were enveloped in a soft cocoon that protected you from any external physical influences. It was nice and warm, and food was always available. You could sleep or relieve yourself whenever you felt like it. You didn't have a concern in the world. You probably perceived this all-round care in the womb as a veritable paradise. In this protected state, you could enjoy your existence in peace and harmony.

Your NES still remembers this feeling today. When you can create situations for yourself that resemble life in the womb, you will feel especially happy (carefree). This is why you should be sure that you are able to regularly spend time in places that are protected, warm, cozy, and, above all, peaceful.

Take time on a regular basis to get as far away as possible from external stimuli.

Having a home of your own would be especially beneficial for you. If your family situation doesn't allow this, at least create a sacred space for yourself – one where any sort of disturbance is strictly prohibited. For example, a quiet room all your own, where you can retreat and shut out external influences.

It's Friday. From Barbara's perspective, it has been a hard day. There were major problems in the department right next to hers and she also wasn't able to get out for her lunchtime walk. What's more, one of her co-workers was offended because she didn't want to go out with her this weekend. What Barbara is really looking forward to is just an evening in front of the TV. She even had to make up a little white lie to tell her boyfriend, since he has been complaining for weeks that they don't spend enough time together. This little fib, which she hasn't told yet, is really stressing her out – she hates herself for it. Tomorrow, first thing, she will admit to him that she really just wanted to be alone and that's why she lied. She decides she will invite him to come to dinner the very next day.

She took care of the grocery shopping yesterday. It's always been important to her to do her shopping promptly. It makes her very happy when her refrigerator is full. She also always makes sure to have enough bottled water and sweets on hand.

She has painstakingly arranged her place on the sofa in front of the television, lovingly setting the delicacies she has so meticulously prepared around her. She arranges her dessert, some other beverages, and anything else she might need later so that she will only have to leave her beloved sofa for a moment to retrieve them. She adjusts the lighting in the room to create a harmonious atmosphere. She then lights a couple of scented candles and shuts off the doorbell and her cell phone.

Now the evening can begin. Barbara decides to go to the bathroom one more time, just to be on the safe side. These constant interruptions to have go to the bathroom drive her absolutely crazy. She often thinks that Mother Nature should have come up with a better plan.

Finally, she grabs her cozy blanket and settles down between her many soft pillows. First, though, she has to painstakingly smooth out all of the folds. She tugs at the blanket and her clothing until everything is just right. Then she slides back and forth on the sofa for a while, trying to find the most comfortable position. Finally, she finds it.

Suddenly, the moment has arrived.

Perfect harmony. She feels the weight of the world lift from her shoulders. Feelings of happiness begin to overtake her. Her mood is now perfect, and she literally laughs out loud: "It doesn't get any better than this," she hears herself say.

Spending time in nature also comes close to the concept of getting away from external stimuli. Your eyes, ears, and nose don't perceive the kinds of impressions you absorb from nature as typical external stimuli. Your brain classifies them as harmonious and calming rather than disturbing or dangerous (as long as you're not sleeping out in the open in the Amazons!)

As often as you can, get away from street noise, construction site racket, and other non-natural external stimuli.

Remember, too, that it is likely that at least one of your senses is extremely fine-tuned (our example of the camera resolution). This means that your brain has to handle a significantly higher data volume than that of a non-HSP.

So, for instance, if you are at a street festival where there is a huge crowd of people, you will always be in danger of your brain becoming overloaded with enormous amounts of information. This is another thing we often don't notice while we are young. The older you get, however, the clearer it will become to you, that you need to be very protective of your mental apparatus. You will often long to find a quiet corner where most of the external stimuli can be shut out. Kind of like a dad, for instance, who likes to retreat to his basement workshop or the garage to work on his hobby. If we examine this more closely, we can see that it is nothing more than a longing for one's own protected space, away from irritating external stimuli. Men who like nothing more than to disappear for days on end to putter around in their workshops are usually also HSPs.

This means that having your own home, or having a room, finished basement, or attic for yourself would provide the ideal conditions for allowing you, at least for a time, to withdraw from the world.

Having a place to retreat to is a matter of survival for HSPs.

If you are a salaried employee, it can be extremely difficult to occasionally get away from your desk. Although there are some broad-minded companies out there who have already installed quiet rooms for their employees, these are the exception to the rule. Still, you will find it very difficult to function if you do not have a physically separate workspace.

Speak to your employer about your need for a quiet atmosphere in the workplace.

If you have the good fortune to work alone (independently) in a laboratory, IT department, office, shop, etc., then this will be very beneficial for you. If, however, you still have to work with a large number of co-workers, managers, or other people, it is critically important that the interactions be peaceable and friendly. At the very least, the relationships need to be neutral, with no negativity.

3.3 THE MAINSTREAM

I'm sure you will agree with me that it has become incredibly difficult to break away from the mainstream. The internet has had the effect of more-or-less synchronizing identical values across the entire globe. An artificial zeitgeist, manufactured by marketing strategists, has permeated to even the farthest reaches of our daily lives. Social media, in particular, continuously confronts us with other people's concepts about life that lead us to quickly doubt whether we are doing the right thing in our own lives.

No previous generation has ever experienced such an extreme bombardment of different life concepts.

Consequently, if you are slim, trim, and attractive, have at least one academic degree, live in your own home (or penthouse apartment) in a hip major metropolitan area, have a family, including an attractive spouse or partner and highly intelligent children, and, on top of all this, can afford regular vacations that take you to the far ends of the earth, then you are regarded as being successful, at least from a societal perspective. In a manner of speaking, you are optimally positioned to have a sense of belonging. If you also happen to hold a highly regarded professional position, all the better.

If your life goals include looking like a fashion model, taking frequent vacations abroad, having an amazing family and a six-figure income, you should check to see if these desires are truly your very own.

If you, as an HSP, were to fall into the trap of being tempted to chase after societal norms that are not truly your own, this would have a profound negative effect on your goal of finding your vocational calling.

Please don't forget: You are striving for FREEDOM and INDEPENDENCE. If you allow yourself to succumb to too many desires that other people have dreamed up or if you fall for some sort of marketing strategy, you will be in danger of binding yourself up in chains of your own making. It will then take years for you to DISENTANGLE yourself. The effort to extricate yourself from this situation could ultimately rob you of your last ounce of vitality. I hope, therefore, that you currently find yourself in a situation in life where you can act and make decisions freely, and that you haven't drifted into any negative situation where your independence is compromised (for example, a mortgage that is too high).

Try to assess which of your desires truly are your own and which have only arisen through the influence of others.

As an HSP, you are especially vulnerable while you are still young. Since, as a young adult, you don't yet have both feet planted firmly on the ground, and because it is highly likely that you were already quite insecure as a child and adolescent, you might be inclined to simply wish for the things that everyone else is going after. Along the lines of: *Everyone else wants it, so I will, too ...*

Julia was in her early thirties. Most of her friends already had children, and so did her siblings and her work colleagues. She, however, didn't yet. Her mind was telling her that it was high time for her, too, to start a family. But in her heart, she didn't really feel an urge to do so. And yet, she was becoming visibly unnerved. At parties, everyone always brought their children, and they were always the main topic of con-

versation. She sometimes had the impression that young mothers had nothing else to talk about besides their little darlings. More and more, Julia felt excluded. And then there was her own mother, who kept asking her at every opportunity when she was finally going to be ready.

One day, her best friend showed up and confided to Julia that she, too, was finally pregnant. She was the last of Julia's close friends who still hadn't had a child. Julia rejoiced with her friend and decided that it was finally time to think about having a child.

For five long years, Julia struggled to conceive. Nothing worked. Finally, when she turned 39, she gave up. It seemed it just wasn't meant to be.

Regardless of whether the idea of starting a family applies to you or not, there are other aspects of life where you can get caught up in the whirlwind of the mainstream. If this were to happen, you would most likely constantly have to pretend that you were conforming to all those rules upon which society typically measures success. Keeping up this appearance would be a risky undertaking for you. Your NES would be constantly screaming at you that it didn't want any of that.

Other than nourishment, a baby has no material desires. These develop much later, as the child matures. Only then does it think in terms like: *This is mine and that is yours.*

The concept of comparing of who has more and who has less also comes along much later. Newborns desire only two things: nourishment and a warm place to sleep.

This attitude toward material things is still firmly embedded within you. If you haven't already long since been aware of this about yourself, at the very latest, when you hit mid-life, you will discover that there are very few compromises you would be willing to make just to be able to own more things. Many HSPs think this means they are simply too lazy. If we look more closely, however, this is not entirely correct. It is just the outwardly perceptible expression of your NEWBORN EGO STATE's unique non-material needs.

A part of you prefers to live modestly.

Here, too, we see a conflict brewing for HSPs. On one hand, they need a lot of acknowledgement – including, of course, from society at large – but on the other hand, they can only attain this if they conform to all of society's rules for success.

So, if you are surrounded by too many people who are extremely mainstream, this can be quite challenging for you – especially if you are not properly emotionally *grounded.* Unfortunately, there is only one way to solve this problem:

Develop some sort of "situational hygiene" early in life.

I have deliberately formulated this last sentence in drastic terms. If you, as a highly sensitive person, surround yourself with others who rob you of your energy, all too frequently make you feel unsure of yourself, or subtly suggest that you are not successful, then you are going to need to protect yourself (even if this is going to deeply upset your need for things to be harmonious).

You are not going to have the strength – and certainly not the desire – to constantly have to prove yourself. This runs completely contrary to your nature.

Nonetheless, you are often going to find yourself in conflict with societal norms. And, naturally, this will always revolve around money.

3.4 YOUR INCOME

If you have already set aside some savings, or if you could begin to do so, this would, of course, be ideal. At the very least, your living costs should not be any higher than what you could expect your income to be if you were receiving unemployment benefits (usually around two-thirds of your current net income, depending on which country you live in). This way, if something were to happen to your job, your entire existence wouldn't be threatened.

> Do not spend more than two-thirds of your income.

The other thing that makes this strategy ideal is that you could then take the other one-third of your income and set up an emergency fund for yourself. This would at least reduce your dependency on your job, allowing you to better maintain your INDEPENDENCE and, at the same time, satisfy your NES's need for security.

If you feel it would be difficult to build up a small savings account, then let me once again recommend that you look at cutting back on your expenditures.

> The key to your freedom primarily lies in reducing your spending.

The western industrialized countries, in particular, are defined by the quest for wealth. There, the primary aim is no longer the pursuit of spiritual, social, or ethical values, but rather, the growth of capital.

The issue of money has infiltrated nearly every aspect of our lives. Everything has to have a payoff. Even when it comes to things like social services, the medical system, or cultural matters, everything is dictated by the market. The free interplay between supply and demand has become the universal benchmark. Everything else is secondary to the belief in the market. It is no surprise, then, that a capitalistic world has decided to go into competition with everyone and everything. Only those who beat out the competition for money and influence are assured of survival and security. Groups of nations battle against other groups of nations. Countries against countries. Communities against communities. Corporations against corporations and, ultimately, individuals against individuals. And in the midst of all this, there you sit, a vulnerable HSP, who is probably worried about becoming collateral damage in this battleground scenario.

On top of all this is the impact of interest earnings, which allow capital to grow more rapidly (exponentially) than the rate of increase in salaries (linearly). This has allowed people in affluent countries to create unimaginable fortunes for the next generation to inherit.

Unfortunately, not every HSP belongs to the inheritance generation. Those who don't can only stand by and watch while, today, only the wealthiest families can afford the exorbitant real estate prices or expensive rents in the big cities.

Please understand that, today, our wealth is determined less by our chosen profession than it is by our parental household.

To the greatest extent possible, avoid any attempt to compensate for a lack of wealth by simply working longer hours. If, for instance, you were to now decide to pursue a certain career simply because it would allow you to live in the center of London, New

York, Paris, Stockholm, Munich, or any other affluent world metropolis, this would probably work out for you for a limited period of time. Sooner or later, however, your highly sensitive body would be pushed to its maximum. Please, just leave the prime real estate to the inheritance generation.

Another thing to be extremely cautious about is compensating for a lack of means by taking out a lot of loans. As an HSP, if you don't have a 100% rock-solid plan for paying off your debt, your NES is going to bombard you with feelings of impending danger until the end of your days. You must never forget that you (still) possess a part of your inner being that is very vulnerable.

I hope you have already observed for yourself that this mad consumerism and chasing after more and more money really gets on your nerves. So, if you find yourself still tormented with longings for wealth and success, bid them farewell now – the sooner, the better.

Robert was a successful business executive. He had been head of an advertising agency for over ten years. He and his family always wore the latest fashions and treated themselves three times a year to an expensive club vacation. Their home was impressively furnished, and Robert was considered as brilliant as he was successful. His daily fitness routine and vegan diet kept him trim and healthy, in keeping with the times. He was dedicated to environmental protection, extremely conscious of energy efficiency, and volunteered for an organization that promoted fair trade.

One morning at breakfast, he suffered an epileptic seizure and collapsed right before his family's eyes. The doctors determined that his entire nervous system was on the brink of collapse. It was time to let go. Robert and his wife began to see that they had no longer been living for themselves, but just to keep up with what they felt the times called for. Their house was too big and so was the mountain of debt they had accrued. The leasing costs for their two electric cars were too high and the money they spent for both of their children to attend universities abroad was exorbitant. Robert woke up. He realized that the life he had been living was a sham. His body had told him this loudly and clearly.

Together with his wife, Robert decided that things had to change. First, they instructed their over-indulged children that they were each to find a part-time job. They then sold the house and replaced their electric cars with conventional vehicles from a used car dealer. They rented a cozy home in the countryside and began to once again live as they had when they first met. They still had some money left over from the sale of the house, and since they had been able to reduce their fixed costs to a minimum, they could get by on this for a while.

Gradually, there was also a marked change in their social circle. They lost all of those friends who could not understand their apparent financial reversal, but they gained many more new friends – people who lived life more thoughtfully and intensively. One of these was a neighboring farmer with whom Robert became friends. He offered to lease Robert a plot of land that he could use to farm and bring in some income. He promised to teach him everything he would need to know and to stand by him as he got started. The two men developed an innovative concept for breeding red deer.

Robert began to once again enjoy life to the fullest. Working in the fresh air and in direct contact with nature and animals did him a world of good. For the first time in many years, he felt a renewed sense of genuine happiness.

He had forgotten what it felt like to have a true zest for life.

Perhaps, however, you are one of those people who has already done everything possible to reduce your costs. It's simply not possible for you to set aside one third of your net income – you literally need every cent you earn. You are already financially on the edge, barely scraping by. This is an extremely difficult situation, but here, too, there is a solution. You are going to have to take a different approach to providing your NES with the security it needs. You shouldn't have to go to work every day in the certainty that if something happened to your job, your entire existence would collapse.

What absolutely won't work is to suppress anything. Your NES will always subtly make itself known. You would begin to be nagged by anxieties. So, if you find yourself in this situation, you are going to need a strategy that eliminates your worry about being too financially dependent on a particular job. You can achieve this, not by having cash reserves on hand, but instead, by having people you can call on for help:

Establish a network of allies.

If you aren't able to achieve security through financial means (the two-thirds strategy), then do it through the assistance of others. To do this, you need to learn more about the concept of networking.

Since, as an HSP, you are eventually going to need to rely on allies, mentors, or other helpers anyway, you should get started early in establishing a team of like-minded individuals.

Once you have enough professional allies at your side, you will feel much more secure. If a situation then actually arose where you had to make a career change, you would have already laid the foundation for that. By that time, you will have established enough contacts. This means that once you have built up your professional network, it will only take a few phone calls for you to land a new job. With the knowledge that you can, at any time, pull a new job out of your hat (if that's what you want to do), your subliminal anxiety about job security will be relieved.

Since a discussion on network-building and the security this provides would go far beyond the scope of this book, I simply recommend that you seek out the numerous thought-provoking books on this subject that are available from any bookdealer.

3.5 YOUR ATTITUDE TOWARD YOUR JOB

We are living in a time of job insecurity. Almost any job out there could disappear from one day to the next. Either the company goes bankrupt or is bought out by another company, or your employer decides to once again implement restructuring or rationalization processes. This on-going pressure for change and transformation may be very stressful for your NES. And, since the globalized labor market isn't likely to change any time soon, you should strongly consider changing your attitude toward your job.

Lucas had sole overall responsibility for the laboratory at a large chemical company. Although he didn't hold a managerial position, he enjoyed being in charge. He had everything perfectly arranged so that he felt comfortable in the space, and for years had been coordinating all the work that went on in the labs. He was the point of contact for all of the lab employees and also handled staff scheduling. He was well-respected and well-known for his absolute reliability. In short, the lab ran like a well-oiled machine.

One day, a new boss suddenly arrived on the scene. Unlike with the previous manager, Lucas no longer had free reign. What upset him even more, though, was the way in which his new boss spoke to him. He felt he was being treated disrespectfully. Things eventually devolved into a confrontation. Lucas immediately resigned.

Lucas was now unemployed and the search for a new job was progressing slowly. He had time on his hands all day to reflect on his life. The more he reflected, the worse he felt. Boredom set in.

In less than six weeks, Lucas was overwhelmed by feelings of depression. On top of that, he felt he was not being treated with sufficient respect in the few interviews he had been able to obtain. He especially felt that the HR departments weren't placing enough importance on his many years of experience in his field. What's more, he was being offered salaries so low that it seemed like a deliberate insult. Since he was dead-set against taking a step backwards professionally, he did not accept any of the offers.

Six months later, Lucas finally began his first sessions with a therapist. He was found to also be suffering from chronic stress.

I know that there are some people who literally hate going to work in the morning. Many of them are just about ready to throw in the towel. If this sounds familiar to you, I would advise you to be extremely cautious. I have rarely seen cases where making a hard break has actually led to improvement in a person's life – quite the contrary. Here, too, you must try to strike a balance.

No matter what, don't give up a regular paycheck if you don't already have the next job in your pocket.

I must tell you, however, that your secret desire to be free and INDEPENDENT will always stand in opposition to taking on a salaried position. Wanting to do your own thing is simply an integral part of being an HSP.

The idea of just throwing it all in and finally doing things on your own is, of course, quite enticing. Until your INTUITION (business sense) is fully functional, however, any entrepreneurial venture or comparable activity would be quite risky. I tell you this for a good reason. I have counseled far too many HSPs in the past who have seen their businesses crash and burn. They were then faced with mountains of debt, physical collapse, or deep feelings of resignation.

At least until the time when you are standing rock-firm with both feet on the ground, I advise you to proceed very cautiously when it comes to self-employment.

No boss in the world can be tougher or more unfair than a customer or a bank.

And this is precisely the clientele you will have to deal with if you run your own business. Your entire existence would be centered around having to cope with this on a daily basis.

If you are feeling as though your current employer isn't treating you fairly or doesn't ACKNOWLEDGE you enough, I can assure you that this situation will be even worse if you become self-employed. At the very least, you have more freedom as an employee (with the proper attitude toward your job) than do many entrepreneurs. And only as an employee can you swap out employers when one doesn't suit you. Once you are self-employed, you will have to attain a very high level of success before you can allow yourself to do the same with a customer or a bank.

Even if the company you work for were to go bankrupt because it just couldn't survive in today's highly competitive market, you, as an employee, could just move on to the next job. If your own business goes bankrupt, however, this can completely wipe you out financially.

I don't want to frighten you unnecessarily, but I also don't want to encourage you to frivolously embark on an entrepreneurial adventure. Treat the idea of self-employment with the great respect it deserves and everything will be fine.

In the end, if your fondest dream is to ultimately become self-employed, I have the utmost understanding for this. This desire is quite simply embedded in your very being. I myself have been self-employed for over twenty-five years now, and although there have been many highs, there have also been some lows. And still, I wouldn't trade my self-employed status for anything in the world. This is primarily because:

If you work for yourself, it will never feel like you're working.

Whether you want to open your own business, look for a job at a new company, or simply determine the right professional attitude to take toward your current job, one thing is very important:

While you are in the LETTING GO phase, never take frivolous risks.

This is especially important for you as an HSP. You simply KNOW too much. Your keen imagination will be able to torment you with the most horrible worst-case scenarios possible. Your sensitive nature is not cut out for this. This means that, sometimes, having a salaried position can initially be a good compromise – at least while you are in the LETTING GO phase. Nevertheless, there are still some serious risks inherent in working for someone else:

HSPs have a tendency to sacrifice themselves to their jobs.

As a rule, HSPs are top performers on the job – they feel a personal responsibility for everything, and they work to ensure that all of the business operations run smoothly. They even go so far as to make constant recommendations for optimizations or ways to make the company more successful. HSPs are ready to go the extra mile if it will benefit the company. Of course, this also ties into their desire be ACKNOWLEDGED, but many people don't even realize that what they are actually doing is acting out their longing to be an entrepreneur.

You could even turn over sole responsibility for the entire company to an HSP – they would basically run the company as if it were their own.

If you also fall into the category of people who have adopted this self-destructive attitude toward their jobs, let me give you some well-intended advice:

Don't play the entrepreneur
when you are just an employee.

Either open your own business and actually live out your desire to be the boss or break yourself of this paradoxical attitude toward your job.

I want to save you from inevitable deep disappointment. As an employee, you are never going to be ACKNOWLEDGED in the way you so fervently desire. Our economic system isn't designed that way. Acknowledgement is shown in a completely different way:

In our economic system, a company
expresses its gratitude by depositing your
salary in your bank account.

That's all. I know this is a sobering and unpleasant thought for many people. But you shouldn't mistake your job for something that, in our capitalist economy, it was never intended to be. Your job is not meant to be a form of therapy that supplies you with love and attention. Unless you have done them a favor, your employer is not required to thank you for your work. You won't be paid extra for doing anyone a favor, though – favors don't usually involve financial reward. And I certainly hope you don't want to be performing unpaid work for your employer! Even if what I am about to say makes you want to send me on a one-way trip to the moon right about now: You are going to have to choose between money and love.

Don't worry, though – I really do completely understand how you feel when all you get is a paycheck and don't receive any other acknowledgement or attention for your work. This is because I know that your NES has triggered a deep-seated conviction in you that there must be someone out there who will take care of you. And so, your NES views the random deposit of your salary as a ridiculous meaningless event.

Adopt a different attitude toward your job. Develop a sense of gratitude that there is someone out there who shares some of their money with you – in the form of a regularly occurring deposit to your bank account.

Thanks to your employer, you have a regular influx of capital without having to take on any sort of existential business risk. Please accept this as being a good deal for both you and your employer. Later, if *you* are in the position of being a business owner, you will better understand this admittedly difficult-to-swallow concept.

Perhaps, though, you are one of the lucky few whose job actually does provide them, in addition to their salary, with acknowledgement and attention. This is then a doubly good deal for you. Someone else is financing your life without you having to take any risks yourself and, on top of that, your need to be ACKNOWLEDGED is being fulfilled. Learn to appreciate this, because in today's working world, this kind of constellation is becoming increasingly rare.

Remind yourself regularly that you are at risk of completely overextending yourself just to attract more attention. You would even go so far as to volunteer to work overtime or take on another huge project. Not only do you tend to think about your job day and night, but you are also capable of performing superhuman feats. And you do all of this with a body that is likely being constantly doped with its own endogenous stress hormones.

Aggravating all of this is your aforementioned tendency toward PERFECTIONISM. Unfortunately, you also KNOW what PERFECT job performance looks like. It's possible you may even be given assignments where it is obvious from the start that no one is ever going to be able to deliver an optimal result. Only you as an HSP would hit upon the terrible idea that you wanted to achieve precisely that. And it is also highly probable you will succeed: delivering PERFECT results on an assignment that was previously thought to be impossible. But now, the next insane project is already pre-programmed, because your boss doesn't even realize that the last assignment should never actually have been possible.

And then there's another problem: You probably aren't going to want to shine a spotlight on your exceptional job performance. After all, you place great value on modesty and restraint. This makes it difficult, though, for your boss or your co-workers to realize that you are actually doing the work of two people. You may grumble a bit while you're doing it, but in the end, everything will be get done – the way it always does. Just at your expense. Your boss and colleagues, on the other hand, will think: *It worked out after all – apparently, it wasn't very difficult. We can definitely add some additional tasks to this person's list.*

If you belong to the self-destructive species of employees I mentioned earlier, it is high time you started protecting yourself from yourself. Recognize that you are secretly acting out your inner desire to be the employer. You are actually taking on the role of an entrepreneur, just without the business license. The company does not belong to you. If your self-sacrifice goes unacknowledged or if you were to lose your job, this could pull the rug right out from under you.

Here, too, you need to change your attitude to your job. Perhaps it would help if, from now on, you began to look at your employer from a different angle. Try to change your perspective:

View your employer as simply a customer.

This means you should think of your job performance as a product that you "sell" to your employer every day. You should actually think of yourself as a service provider. This would make your employer simply your client, who "purchases" the work you perform. Your salary represents your monthly business revenue. In practical terms, since your boss would be your client, this would mean that you have just one single client. Everyone else that you have to interact with at your workplace is *no longer your* customer, but that of *your client* instead.

By taking this attitude toward your job, you could at least indirectly live out your desire to be an entrepreneur. Although you are still an employee, in your own mind, you are the owner of a one-person business. At the same time – as a sort of dry run – you could test out what entrepreneurial thinking really involves.

When you want to sell a service, there is always a calculation that must be made. You have to look at the relationship between your costs and the price you can charge. Your sales revenue is represented by the salary you receive as an employee. Your costs include your nerves and your time as well as your tolerance for senseless work assignments.

With this new perspective in mind, you should now take a fresh look at your job: What portion of the services you provide in your daily work still pays off? Is what you deliver each day on the job completely covered by your selling price (your salary) or are you selling your services below cost? If so, you are going to have to make a recalculation (otherwise, you are going to be at the end of your rope – either financially or psychologically).

Do a cost-benefit analysis. Either your client (your employer or your boss) is going to have to pay you more (which is very unlikely) or, as a responsible business owner, you are going to have to adjust your costs (nerves, time, senseless work, etc.) to fit to your sales revenue (salary). It may be that, because your own costs are too high, from now on, your client (your boss) is going to have to accept a compromise when it comes to the quality of your work. Perhaps you will also no longer be able to tend to your client's customers to the extent you have in the past, because the payoff for you isn't worth it and, at the end of the day, they are *his* or *her* customers and not yours.

While you are still employed, begin thinking like an entrepreneur.

When you attempt to internalize this attitude, however, you will find yourself confronted with yet another major challenge in your PERSONAL GROWTH. Just the fact alone that, based on your salary or the actual physical demands of your job, you are adjusting your commitment to your job downward is going to awaken a feeling of dread in you. You are now going to feel that you are not doing your job correctly.

Overcome your panic that you are doing something wrong.

If you aren't able to do this, you will be missing out on one of the most important tools you have for molding your boss to your advantage. Your co-workers have probably long since figured out how to avoid extra work. Only you, the HSP, have probably not.

If you are being overloaded with too much work, you need to penalize your boss or your co-workers for this by delivering work that is less than perfect. This is the only way to protect yourself from being overburdened by others. If, as an HSP, you are afraid to make use of this *leadership technique for managers*, then, in no time at all, you will be viewed as the person who is literally predestined to take on extra work.

Train yourself to make mistakes.

This will not only reduce your tendency toward excessively achievement-oriented thinking and PERFECTIONISM, but it will also make you aware of something crucial: You will begin to see that making mistakes doesn't have the dramatic negative effect you had previously imagined. It will become clear to you that it was often just you, yourself, who was putting such pressure on you.

Resolve that tomorrow, you are going to be the cause a minor mishap.

Alternatively, you could also just be half an hour late for an important appointment. Or go ahead and think of something else important (in your view) that you could screw up a bit. This little test of your daring is not only more than constructive for your highly sensitive being, it also significantly increases your resilience.

If you were to make a conscious decision to go ahead and make a few mistakes, this would bring with it another nice advantage: You could optimally prepare yourself for this in advance. Even if you were to receive a reprimand (which I doubt), you would be perfectly prepared for this mentally. You could then sit back and calmly observe this type of conflict situation and, above all, also observe yourself. The world is definitely not going to come to an end. You will build up a sort of emotional callus if, now and then, you intentionally deliver results that are merely average (which, from your subjective perspective, means they are flawed) and then calmly observe the reactions of your colleagues or bosses.

What's more, you will be acquiring a powerful tool for yourself: You will be learning how to manage your boss to your advantage if you are once again given a much too heavy workload. More quickly than you can imagine, your boss is going to realize that if they don't act in your best interest, this is going to lead to a slew of mistakes. Don't worry that your boss might complain about you to upper management. If they were to do this, they would be accused of being a weak leader, which would be far more damaging to their future career than simply accepting your new attitude toward your work.

In the end, if none of this applies to you, then consider yourself lucky. If that is not the case, however, then you are going to have to finally come to terms with the fact that you are an employee. You need to develop a professional attitude toward your work that will fit in with today's changing workplace. You need that regular paycheck. If you don't accept your status as an employee as it was actually designed to be, you will be disregarding the needs of your NES.

Of course, it goes without saying that there is a limit to everything. If you are having to tolerate unbearable working conditions, incompetent managers, or a business owner completely lacking in entrepreneurial talent, then, unfortunately, even a change in your attitude isn't going to accomplish much. Then, you are actually going to have to phase this employer out of your life. You can exchange them for a different employer, or you can quickly acquaint yourself with the topic of networking.

3.6 SELF-CENTEREDNESS

As you learned earlier, a certain CLAIM TO LEADERSHIP resides deep within you. Along with this, you also have a somewhat egocentric perspective of the world. As mentioned, this is related to your NEWBORN EGO STATE.

A baby can't move anywhere on its own. It isn't able to look at the world from a variety of perspectives. It isn't yet aware that millions of other babies are also being born. And, it has to ensure that it is the center of attention. After all, its survival is dependent on the people who care for it. It is literally compelled to view the world from an egocentric perspective.

The only tools a baby has at its disposal to protect itself from danger are its powers of observation. Its only hope is to be able to assess a situation faster than anyone else. Then, it can promptly begin to fuss loudly, drawing attention to itself so that help will arrive. This means that simply for reasons of survival, a baby has to relate everything it sees, smells, hears, or feels to itself.

As an HSP, this continues to influence you today. You probably still constantly view everything and everyone in relation to yourself.

> Many HSPs suffer from a high degree of self-centeredness.

In combination with your subtle CLAIM TO LEADERSHIP, this results in a typical HSP extreme: You *always* feel responsible for everything. Of course, this constantly taking responsibility and being involved can also be seen as a noble personality trait – after all, this is precisely the opposite of ignoring something. In your case, however, it can take on a pathological aspect. An overly exaggerated sense of responsibility for your job can quickly result in mental overload. To protect your health, you should observe the following rule, even if you find it difficult:

Please only feel responsible for something when you have explicitly been asked to do so.

So, if you hear about a problem that is happening in the next department over, that is not *your* problem. It isn't necessary (at least in your professional life) to always see yourself as the great protector of the dispossessed, the widows, and the orphans. Also, if one of your co-workers screws up, it's not your fault. And likewise, there is no need to worry that you've done something wrong just because a police car happens to pull up next to you at a red light.

You don't need to worry about everything. You are not to blame!

Please stop over-thinking everything.

I know that this is another suggestion that may make you feel uncomfortable. I'm sure you hate it when your co-workers or your boss don't think things through sufficiently. When they are just too lazy to exert their own brains. After all, this is precisely the kind of thing that has upset you all your life.

I will repeat myself: You are a fragile being. More so than for others, it is virtually essential for you to clear your head of superfluous thoughts. You need to practice more mental self-care.

But don't worry: In putting this into practice, you will still maintain such a high sense of responsibility that you will never need to worry about actually becoming oblivious to those around you. You will still be one of those people who thinks things through thoroughly, but you will do so at a level that doesn't threaten your own health.

Incidentally, your tendency to be overly self-centered can also reveal itself on an entirely different level:

Because it was storming, Susan decided to drive to the office. As she had so often, when she pulled into a spot in the company parking garage, she made sure to leave enough room between her car and the one parked next to her. This way, the other driver would have plenty of room to get in. She hadn't given herself much room on her own side, however. She literally had to squeeze out of the door.

Suddenly, an employee from another department also drove in and parked his car. Susan greeted him with a friendly "Good morning!" Her co-worker, though, didn't respond. Susan didn't call after him, but after she went up to her office, she couldn't stop thinking about the situation. Was there some reason he didn't respond to her greeting? Was something going on that she didn't know about? Had there been a problem with her work this week? Maybe he was mad at her because she hadn't noticed him at some point, and this was just his way of paying her back?

Susan was overwhelmed by countless suppositions about what might have happened. By the time her coffee break came around, her mood had sunk to its lowest point. She didn't exactly know why. And just then, the unfriendly jerk from the office next to hers came through the door and asked if she had the printer cartridges. "Am I responsible for everything around here?" she heard herself snap at him.

During her lunch break, she ran into the co-worker she had seen that morning in the parking garage. He greeted Susan warmly and asked why they hadn't yet bumped into each other that morning – maybe she was just really busy at the moment?

Have a little fun with this. The next time your body decides it must once again prepare itself for mortal combat, flooding you with stress hormones, just start to laugh at yourself. Begin to cut down on the number of these little everyday catastrophes that leave those around you looking at you in disbelief, not sure of what has just happened.

Tell your NEWBORN EGO STATE that it is not a matter of life or death if someone doesn't happen to say hello to you.

Another good example of this would be if you were sitting in your office, working at your computer, and you suddenly heard laughter in the next room. Only you, as an HSP, would come to the conclusion that the others were laughing about you. This bizarre idea would never even occur to a non-highly sensitive person, but to you, it certainly would. Even though just a few seconds earlier you were relaxed and working confidently on the task at hand, in the blink of an eye, your NES was able to transform you into a vulnerable little child.

Another typical example would be a situation in which it was somehow extremely important to you to reduce the number of customer complaints. Your own common sense will have told you that this could only be a positive thing for the company. If you haven't thoroughly discussed the issue with your boss, however, you can't know if this is equally important to them. It's possible that some of the final post-production inspections have been discontinued for optimization reasons and that a conscious decision has been made to accept the higher error rate. It may be that even though correcting the errors after the fact entails some unpleasant customer complaints, it is financially more advantageous than performing the checks that keep the production process error-free. It may also be that upper management is actually requiring your boss to do this, and that he or she is just putting a good face on the situation.

And it could be that it is actually clear to everyone except you that all of the numerous customer complaints are going to have to be accepted as a necessary evil.

So here you now come with your subjective view of the matter and annoy your boss with your suggestions on how to prevent production errors. And that's not all: Perhaps you don't accept your boss's explanations as to why the situation isn't so bad, and HARD-HEADEDLY stick to your opinion (and being HARD-HEADED generally results in a HEADACHE). After all, you are only trying to do what is in the company's best interest.

If you are this kind of an extremely subjective person, no matter how hard you work, those around you will eventually view you as being annoying. Not to mention that your strong desire to be ACKNOWLEDGED will certainly be thwarted. From your perspective, you believe you are doing your job PERFECTLY, but, as an HSP, you also very clearly sense that there is negativity in the air. And it is in the nature of things that in this situation, you won't be able to enjoy your work.

Train yourself to see things through the eyes of others.

A final example would be something that happens in so many family-owned businesses. Frequently, the owners are second- or third-generation family members whose financial well-being has long since been secured. Their fathers or grandfathers were able to stockpile sufficient capital and their private investment holdings have been established for years. There is no existential urgency for these executives to exert themselves to ensure the sustainable success of their family business. They are often more concerned with pursuing their hobbies, finding their purpose in life, spending time with their families, etc. Their interest lies more in making sure that life as the company's top executive is stress-free and pleasant. If you fail to recognize this, it could mean a swift end to your career.

If, for example, you were to constantly come up with new ideas for increasing company profits, but these would entail more work for the CEO, you could very quickly become *persona non grata.* From your perspective, you are being an exemplary employee, attempting to ensure the sustainable growth of the company. In the eyes of top management, however, you are simply becoming a pain in the backside. If you were to take an interest in your boss's true desires, however, and keep employees, customers, and anyone else from disturbing them, you would soon be considered irreplaceable. Before you knew it, you would be enjoying professional perks that might even make you forget about the issue of your true vocational calling.

3.7 SELF-PROMOTION

The idea of putting on an act to obtain some sort of advantage or another is something you completely reject. Such self-promotion is contrary to your natural honesty – not to mention that you aren't any good at it. Once again, the reasons for this can be found in your not-yet-feeling-secure NES.

Newborns don't yet have the ability to hide behind a mask. They are the living embodiment of HONESTY. Not until much later will they learn to pretend, to take on a role, or to consciously change their behavior in order to obtain something. Their first little acts of dishonesty will appear, at the latest, once they enter school. Then, children start to make up lies to explain to the teacher why they haven't done their homework or why they are late to class. Not to even mention making little cheat sheets or copying their neighbor's answers so that they can pass the math test.

Later, we begin our professional lives, and at that point our honesty truly comes to an end. We even learn how to lie professionally: Patients, customers, guests, suppliers, or the boss will all be promised the moon and the stars. We make up stories about being sick. The customer on the other end of the line is told that the computer just crashed. We lie to the boss about why we have to leave early. Or the potential guest is informed that there are currently no rooms available. Lying becomes as natural as breathing.

When employees finally make their way up the career ladder and take on their first managerial positions, the end of the line is nowhere near yet in sight. Quite the contrary: Now is when the many little (or even bigger) deceptions really get underway. Top management puts pressure on middle management to break one law or another. Decision-makers have to sign off on things that do not reflect reality, or they have to fudge statistics, or put their names to falsified information. Deceiving customers, their own employees, and, above all, themselves, becomes a part of the daily routine.

As an HSP, this sort of situation will be very difficult for you to tolerate. You want to behave fully in accordance with your ideal of HONESTY. Your highly developed conscience actually forces you to do so.

To your way of thinking, even harmless little tricks carried out to gain a few minor advantages count as deception. You are not cut out to take part in some underhanded little game. Even when it sometimes is necessary to tell a little white lie, this is written all over your face. All in all, it is exceptionally important to you to be honest – you simply can't be any other way.

HSPs are incapable of playing a particular part just to put themselves at an advantage in life.

Sadly, in many cases, this is exactly what is required to get ahead professionally in these times of declining values. This explains why so many highly sensitive people get stuck in the lower hierarchical levels of a firm or never earn more than a mediocre salary. They are just repelled by the idea of power struggles, strategic game-playing, or shameless self-promotion as a means to career success.

Now, a danger lurks: You might decide to compensate for your distaste of blatant self-promotion with your high-performance mindset. In other words, to move up the career ladder, you might strive to work harder and better than everyone else – something that would, however, inevitably lead to the chronic stress and mental overload that has been previously discussed. You can only avoid this conflict by taking an alternative approach:

Place more emphasis on your feelings than on your performance.

Rather than your performance, your emotions could be the key to gaining more ACKNOWLEDGEMENT. You need to recognize that it is often not your job performance that determines how much attention you receive or that boosts you up the career ladder, but your ability to make yourself seen.

Try to live more authentically.

This will also help you slowly but surely dismantle the emotional wall you have undoubtedly built up around yourself all your life. Experience has shown that *this* will also be especially difficult, since, after all, your inner vulnerability means that you have a lot to lose.

And yet, there is no other way around it. At some point you are going to have to LET GO of your aloofness. You are wasting too much energy and mental effort trying to suppress your emotional state (or not let it show). This often means that others aren't sure who you really are, which leads to them not having a sense of trust in you. This drastically increases the danger that you will become the target of a bullying campaign. Then, you can work until you drop, and you are still never going to advance in your career.

As you know, other people not only perceive you visually (see you) and auditively (hear you), but also – and primarily – on a deeper emotional level. It is this last level that is always involved in communication. This means that when what other people see or hear from you lines up with what they feel from you, it produces a sort of "emotional unambiguousness." You might say that you are then "easy to read." You radiate authenticity. Other people can clearly judge for themselves whether you are benign or represent a threat.

Incidentally, it doesn't matter at all which conclusion the other person comes to. The only thing that matters is that they can clearly assess who and what you are. This allows them to decide whether or not they need to take defensive measures. They are then prepared and know what to do. They simply feel safe around you.

Now, I'm going to assume that you're not intending to do anything that endangers your boss or your co-workers in any way. That means that your intentions are purely innocent. It is still possible, however, that for the reasons mentioned earlier, others may react to you in an overly cautious manner.

Tear down your emotional protective wall.

If you don't do this, everyone you work with will be kept standing outside this emotional wall. This will create an ambiguous emotional situation for them. They won't be able to clearly size you up and faster than you can imagine, they will start taking defensive measures against you. You, on the other hand, will be utterly bewildered, because with your high-performance mindset and perfectionism, you can't imagine that you have done anything wrong. As an HSP, however, you will immediately sense that people are reacting warily to you – and it may not yet be clear to you that at such moments, you don't come across as particularly likeable to the others.

When there is a discrepancy between what you feel and what you are saying, this not only puts a strain on you – it also makes you seem unlikeable.

This brings us back to the advice I've already given you: Letting your feelings out is the *fastest* way to *relieve the strain* on your brain. And now, there is even an additional benefit. If you behave more authentically, not only do you significantly reduce the danger of burnout, but you also appear to be a nicer person.

Now you can probably also understand the secret to being seen as a likeable person. There are people out there who constantly put their foot in their mouths, make one mistake after the other, or, in extreme cases, even openly flaunt their own stupidity or uncouthness, and still, everyone likes them. These people are simply authentically being themselves. They aren't hiding their inner feelings. They are so emotionally unambiguous that no one feels at all threatened by them.

Never underestimate other people's intuition. If your actions don't reflect your feelings, this will set off the alarm bells in other people's subconscious minds. You will then be met with distrust – sometimes even with aggression. And the result will be just the opposite of what you, with your intense need for harmoniousness and your performance mindset, are trying to achieve. Being rejected or attacked is the worst thing that could happen to you. And it will only have happened because you didn't trust people enough to tear down your emotional wall beforehand.

It goes without saying that here too, of course, there are boundaries that must be respected. Naturally, it is sometimes helpful to maintain a certain unapproachability. If this becomes a permanent condition, however, not only are you going to have difficulty integrating yourself professionally and moving ahead with your career, but it is also going to cost you far too much mental energy.

You are certainly not going to be able to change every pattern of behavior overnight. Especially not if your NES is still battling mightily inside you with its fears. But you can take things one step at a time.

Starting now, gradually begin to synchronize your feelings with your behavior.

This means that when you're happy to see someone, show them. When you're irritated, don't act as though everything is fine. And when you're in a bad mood, don't try to pretend otherwise.

I am aware that, especially for HSPs, every new contact brings with it new emotional challenges. The risk of being hurt is simply too high. You can't yet properly size up the other person. Rejection or disrespect may be imminent.

Still, you should try to overcome your emotional anxiety and begin to more and more frequently allow people to see your true feelings. Of course, this doesn't mean that you should go blabbing the intimate details of your life to your co-workers. You can simply start with benign topics:

- Tell a story about something that recently happened to you outside of work.
- Share some information about your family.
- Let people know how you feel about certain things.
- Share your personal perspective on current events.

The degree to which you want to give others a glimpse into who you are is determined by your willingness to take risks. Usually, the further you go, the more the other person will open up to you.

When you act more authentically in your professional environment, top-performance results are no longer necessary.

Perhaps in the past, you could never understand why some of your colleagues got promoted up the career ladder even though their work couldn't begin to measure up to yours. Now you probably understand why – because it rarely is about PERFECT job performance.

To cut to the chase: Try to be a little braver and share more of your feelings with other people. When your external behavior halfway matches up with your inner emotions, you become visibly authentic to others. You seem nicer and more likeable. What will happen then is that others will drop their cautious attitudes toward you and react more positively to you. People will start to like you more, and this will do your soul a world of good. This way, you can also avoid getting involved in power plays or having to engage in over-inflated self-promotion, while still increasing your chances for improving your income, advancing your career, or simply being given better working conditions.

3.8 SOURCES OF STRESS

We're getting near the end of this chapter on LETTING GO. As you have no doubt noticed, nearly all of the recommendations I have made center around one specific issue:

> You need to protect your mind from constant stress.

Remember our comparison of the brain to the engine of a Formula 1 racecar? This engine is exclusively designed to operate at top performance for the limited duration of the race. Before and after this, it must be vigilantly cared for and maintained. You certainly aren't going to take your sports car to run your daily errands. And so it is with your brain. It was designed to provide you with strokes of absolute genius, but only for limited periods of time. Outside of this time, it needs peace and rest. If instead, you are overloading it 24/7, you are, in practical terms, burning out your high-performance mental apparatus. You are using it for something it was never designed to do.

This means that you are absolutely physically capable of doing hard work (just like non-HSPs). You simply have to organize your private and professional lives in such a way that you are protected from PERMANENT overload. What is key here is LETTING GO of constant fears about the future, taking on too many duties, constant worrying, striving for harmony, or a lack of boundaries.

On the whole, this kind of permanent stress is usually brought on by general types of conflicts – the contradictions between reality and your plans or other ideas. If you were to more deeply analyze these emotional stressors, you would notice something much more basic. You would become aware that that the primary cause for this stress is unnecessary thought processes having to do with your future. If you would keep your thoughts in the present moment, they could never lead to a mental overload:

Your genius is exclusively designed for the here and now.

You literally hate being forced to think about tomorrow. Essentially, you don't want to have to think about whether you have enough money to get through the rest of the month or if your job is still going to be there next year. You would greatly prefer to let others worry about the future. And there is a very specific reason for this:

You have a deep-seated need for timelessness.

Again, this aspect of your being can be explained by the description of a newborn: Babies are absolutely aware of the passing of time. They recognize quite early that when they hear Mommy singing a little song, they are being fed or diapered. Or they are aware of certain things their father is doing that tell them: *Ok, that is the signal that it's time to sleep.* They understand, too, that when they want to play or when they are hungry, Mommy and Daddy spend time with them. They are aware of certain time-related relationships, but this is just the first step in understanding the phenomenon of time. At this point, it is more about the associations that are linked to the moment.

For instance, it's not possible to teach a baby that a certain signal it receives today means it will have a bath tomorrow. Newborns have no concept of the future.

Not until much later, when they are two or three years old, do children develop a sense of what is referred to as social time. At this age, for example, children can understand that Sunday is the special day when the family goes out for ice cream. In the years that follow, more complex time tasks will be mastered. Children can then understand that another two weeks will have to go by before it is their birthday and they will receive their presents.

All of this affects your NES to a very high degree. This part of your ego will react with confusion and fear if external factors literally force you to have to give too much thought to the future.

You can only feel truly content when you are living in the here and now.

There will certainly be times when you wish that you could simply shut your mind off. However, your AES (in other words, you yourself) will fight this. You are going to always have a tendency to want to plan and control things. This means that you have to provide yourself (in other words, your intellect) with a few cold hard facts so that it will quit doing this, practically of its own accord.

Minimize the number of occasions where you are forced to have to think about the future.

I'm sure you will agree with me that this is an especially high hurdle to have to clear. You will, of course, never be able to completely eliminate these thought processes. However, this is also not necessary. It is only the conflict-associated thoughts that you need to make disappear. And this is exactly what will happen if you put all of the guidance in the previous sub-chapters into practice.

In addition to that guidance, I'd like to conclude this chapter with a few more tips on how to create a more stress-free life for yourself. For instance, one good way to do this would be to establish a daily structure. If you don't have to spend the evening planning for the next day because you've already established a structure for it, this will help fulfill your desire to not have to think about time. This will be especially easy for HSPs with a young family, since children also appreciate having a predictable routine.

You need things in your environment
to be predictable.

This should also be something you strive for at the workplace. If you have a job where each new day holds unpredictable surprises or your working rhythm is constantly thrown into chaos, this is definitely not the ideal situation for your highly sensitive personality. If you find yourself in such a situation, my advice to you is:

Be sure to plan extra time to deal with
surprises into your workday.

In other words, develop an inner acceptance of potential interruptions. Be mentally prepared ahead of time that you may have to improvise.

Today, you have be ready to cope with constantly changing work conditions. This can be learned. So, although this constant change is certainly not ideal for you, you will make it even worse if you take a *hard-headed* approach to it. It is often not the chaos itself that leads to stress, but our refusal to accept it.

Plan ahead for the unpredictable. A nasty surprise that you've anticipated isn't a surprise anymore. You should also use some kind of time planner in which you can note all of your appointments and your to-do list (a smart phone, computer, pocket calendar, etc.)

Every item you write down is one less thing you have to remember.

Don't worry that this is going to lead your brain to become lazy. You are an HSP. Your intellectual abilities are already at their peak.

Make appointments with yourself, too, for specific times you want to think about certain things. The less you have to carry around in your head, the better. This way you can free up your brain's capacity to take on more important tasks, like creative thinking (or brilliant ideas).

If you already use this type of time management system for your job, then you only need to make a daily to-do list. This means that you no longer have to spend time in the evening thinking about what you need to do the next day, because all you need to do is look at your list (which will also include the time buffer you've set up for those unexpected little surprises.)

This kind of a to-do list not only saves mental effort, but, above all, it helps you get your work done more quickly so that you can enjoy your evenings. If there is something you didn't get to that day, simply carry it over to the next day or the day after that. You can then let it evaporate from your mind. You can rest assured that the next time you work your way down your to-do list, you're going to be reminded of it anyway.

Many HSPs also keep a journal. They find that this not only helps them to better structure their thoughts, but that is also a wonderful form of meditation.

3.9 PUTTING IT ALL TOGETHER

Whenever problems, conflicts, or other difficulties arise in your life, you should always apply the LETTING GO techniques.

I'm sure that for some of my readers, the suggestions I have made sound a bit overwhelming. I've also given you a picture of reality that most likely sounds far too sobering. All of this is intentional on my part.

It is better for you to mentally make your peace with the world I have described and then perhaps be positively surprised now and then than it would be for you to chase after some overly sentimental notion of the world only to be faced with one disappointment after the other.

There is no calculated pessimism whatsoever in this basic approach to life – it simply serves to increase your emotional resilience. Most of all, it will allow you to reach a stage in your PERSONAL GROWTH where the entire bandwidth of your ingenuity will be evident. The sacrifice you make in LETTING GO of some of your preconceptions of life will seem almost ridiculously small in comparison to what awaits you. Only in hindsight will you be able to see the value of having gone down some of these arduous paths.

In the majority of cases, HSPs only have to shoulder this burden once in their lives before they experience how, as if by magic, everything resolves itself.

Incidentally, many HSPs have also made their lives a little happier by deciding to befriend their NES. They think of it as a separate entity. They admit, in embarrassment, that they even sometimes speak to it in the third person (*Don't be like that. Yes, I've already noticed that, too. It's not going to be so bad.).* I personally think that this is an amusing technique for keeping things from getting too serious. Not taking yourself or life too seriously is a good first step to making peace with the here and now and all of its paradoxical contradictions.

Getting back to LETTING GO – essentially, you have two options for doing this: You can either change your attitude or you can change your environment.

> If something can be changed, change it. And if it cannot be changed, then learn to accept it.

The speed with which you progress will depend on how far you go in dealing with the topics that have been covered:

1. Taking Breaks
2. External Stimuli
3. The Mainstream
4. Your Income
5. Your Attitude Toward Your Job
6. Self-Centeredness
7. Self-Promotion
8. Sources of Stress

The act of LETTING GO actually represents an intermediate step in your PERSONAL GROWTH. This means that finding your vocational calling is not going to be the solution to all of your personal and professional problems, but, conversely, that once you have resolved these problems, you will find your true vocational calling. I know that this sounds like another paradox.

But at this point, you should be able to well understand why this is the only way it works.

You have learned that your HES not only works while you are sleeping, but, especially, that it only works when you are living a life that is at least halfway carefree. In other words, when your brain isn't so overloaded that it overlooks the intuitive information coming from your HES.

And please don't forget: If your intuition is not functioning fully and correctly, you are practically stuck in a rut, because your highly sensitive body was specifically designed to pursue an INTUITIVELY LED LIFE. This is the true purpose of your highly sensitive existence.

The further away from this you are, the more difficult it will be. At the same time, I want to emphasize here that there is no point in thinking about simply dropping out of the system completely. The backwaters of this world are full of highly sensitive dropouts who, in deep disappointment, have simply turned their backs on real life. These despairing people will probably never find a way to make peace with reality. In Christianity, they would be thought of as lost souls: hard-headed, stubborn people who have utterly lost their connection to their intuition and thus, to the INVISIBLE WORLD. They then become fair game for psychics, gurus, charlatans, marketing experts, or anyone else out to steal their souls.

You, on the other hand, now know better. There is no need for you to become a drop-out. You just need to show a little humility, change some of your attitudes toward life, and disentangle yourself from whatever is holding you back.

If you now remind yourself that you are, by nature, someone who likes to develop new things (see Chapter 2), then you will also know the very first step you have to take on the path to your vocational calling. You yourself have to undergo a development.

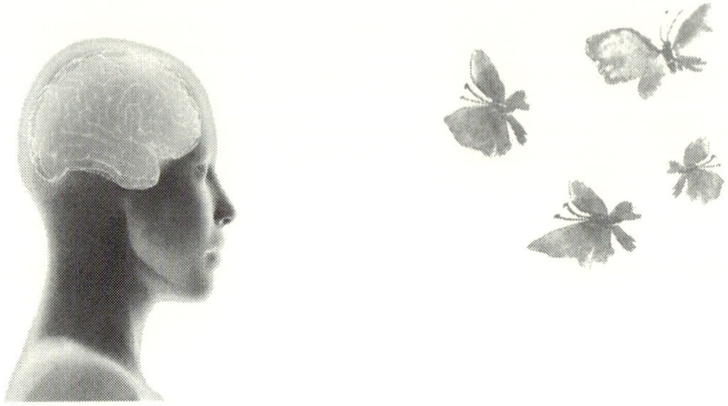

Before you can develop anything else,
you must first work on your own development.

Even if your AES is not yet fully absorbing the information your HES is sending it, your HES is still there. Your intuition will be providing your AES with at least a minimum amount of KNOWLEDGE. Usually, this means that you also KNOW for yourself from experience which areas of your life you need to work on. You really don't even need anyone else's advice – you know where the problems lie.

Perhaps it was even your INTUITION that led you to this book. That would mean that right now might just be the perfect moment for you to develop a solution to one of your problems.

—

Stop now for just a moment and take a deep breath!

Whatever your first thought was – this is precisely the first conflict that needs to be resolved or let go of.

Write down what your first thought was:

....

....

....

....

....

....

Hang a note with this thought on your bathroom mirror. Every morning, it will serve as a reminder and help you combat your tendency to very efficiently suppress the thought of any existing conflicts. You could basically put this book down right now and get to work.

From this point on, everything in this book will be about your future. And thinking about this too soon could actually be counterproductive. You might even come up with the (bad) idea of taking the second step before you've taken the first.

It is, however, also absolutely conceivable that you are one of those people who has long since put all of the aspects discussed so far into practice. If you are in this group, it's time to move forward. New questions are going to emerge. It's no longer simply a matter of fulfilling the prerequisites for finding your vocational calling – now you will be actually setting off on your concrete search. Things are about to really get going.

Part B

The Future

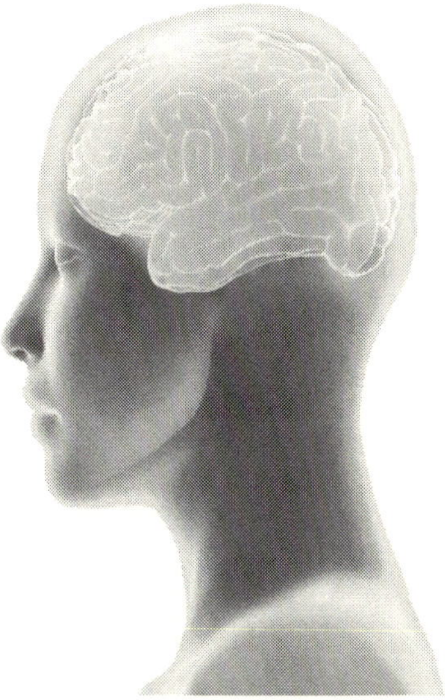

IMPORTANT NOTE:

Until the concepts in the chapter "What Do I Need to Do to Let Go?" have been effectively put into practice, any attempt at the practical application of the information that follows could result in overwhelming stress.

4 When Do I Most Enjoy My Job?

It's only natural for you to feel content when you've made yourself comfortable in your sheltered space (your living room) and have some yummy treats at hand. You've actually artificially created a situation in which you feel safe and protected. If you've also made sure that you can forget about everything else until tomorrow, many peaceful moments will be yours to enjoy.

However, if this were to become your daily routine for months (or years) on end, these feelings of contentment would gradually give way to boredom, which you'd likely find rather distressing.

You'll become aware that something is missing, and you'll want to break out of your routine. Perhaps you'll turn to your computer, video games, or even just your television, for distraction. Or you may try to relieve your boredom with special foods or alcoholic drinks. However, this won't last for long either.

You are once again dealing with an extreme. Once you have achieved inner peace, another threat begins to loom. Because you are now under-stimulated, you may be overtaken by feelings of gloominess. Not caused by a burnout (an overload) in this case, but instead, from a "bore-out" (an "underload").

In general, feelings of boredom are a helpful signal that it is slowly time to start turning your attention to finding your vocational calling.

So, feeling bored is not necessarily a bad thing. It proves that you are still on the right path. This is also better than being in despair, since feelings of distress would be a sign that you were trying to fight your way through the thorny brush on the side of that path – in other words, you were about to veer off your life path for good. If your *only* problem is that you are bored, then you are still on the straight and narrow. You've just gotten somehow stuck and are going to have to get yourself moving again.

> If you are feeling bored or restless, this is a clear signal that you need to slowly but surely get out of your comfort zone.

Now, it is really time to get going. At this point, you not only should have found the calmness and peace you desire, but it's also time to introduce more fun into your life.

Since feelings of joy naturally also belong to your emotional realm, we are going to continue to keep an eye on your NES. Now, however, your HES – in other words, your intuitive ability – is going to take on an increasingly important role. We are therefore going to take a closer look at the following four aspects:

1. Reactions
2. Self-esteem
3. Variety
4. Understanding

4.1 REACTIONS

Highly sensitive people are usually not the type to wear their feelings on their sleeves. Exuberant greetings and other emotional displays tend to put them off. Especially during the first half of their lives, they are inclined to remain more aloof.

This usually dissipates over the course of their lives, however, as they gradually begin to tear down the emotional walls they've erected. Once you've reached that point, you will notice, however, that a slight bit of that aloofness never goes away. This is also in the nature of things – ultimately, you will still continue to appreciate your "alone time." In addition, with your NES, AES, and HES, you are carrying three ego states around with you, which, generally speaking, can provide you with everything you need. You have someone whom you must constantly protect and care for (NES), someone who does the thinking, working, and living (AES), and someone who provides guidance and shows you the way, who takes care of you and manages everything (HES). From an existential point of view, you don't need anyone else. You have yourself. Nonetheless, you still need to open yourself to the greatest extent possible to your environment. There is a special reason for this:

> To be able to experience more joy in life, you are still dependent on others.

The underlying meaning of this statement is once again to be found in your highly complex emotional realm. You need to take the first step of sensing the feelings of others so that you will then be better able to tune into your own feelings:

Sometimes, you only begin to feel something yourself once you have experienced the feelings of others.

You'll then find yourself sitting at a café just so that you can watch the people passing by. You want (usually unconsciously) to try to read their moods. I know HSPs who absolutely love people-watching. They actually get a real sense of joy out of this passive activity. The reason for this will become obvious if we take another look at our example of the baby.

Newborns have a kind of inborn facial recognition program. They are mainly interested in looking at faces. They don't pay attention to things like clothing, hairstyles, or the like. There is a very simple explanation for this. It has been said that our facial expressions (facial features) are a direct reflection of our emotions. By observing faces, not only is the baby learning to recognize its parents, but it is also learning the difference between different emotional states. Strangers will be checked out, too, to see if they are calm and happy or if danger is looming. The primary thing babies are really doing here, however, is learning just what emotions actually are.

The explanation behind why this works can be found in another natural phenomenon. Not only do our facial expressions change according to our emotions, but it also works the other way around – our facial muscles can actually trigger emotions. Your emotional state is then a reflection of your facial expression and not the other way around.

For instance, if you force yourself to pull your mouth into a big smile, it's impossible to stay in a bad mood while you are doing this.

If you ever find yourself in a bad mood, you can put this to the test yourself. And this is how our emotions get trained while we're very young. If you smile at a baby, it reacts to this and smiles back at you. And this way, the baby experiences for itself the feelings of happiness that come with smiling. In the beginning, babies don't know what friendliness feels like. Not until they have imitated the facial expression of the other person can they experience this feeling. And then these little bundles of joy learn: "Aha! That feels good!" (see "*Emotionale Kompetenz bei Kindern,*" by Franz Petermann and Silvia Wiedebusch).

This is also the reason that adults unconsciously behave somewhat over-dramatically when communicating with newborns (e.g., *oh-oh-oh, biddy-biddy-boo*, and other nonsense sounds). This slightly ridiculous behavior, including greatly exaggerated facial expressions, is nonetheless exactly what babies need. The over-the-top facial expression of emotions makes it easier for babies to more clearly recognize these and imitate them. They can then more quickly learn a variety of emotions.

Let's look again at your NES. It experiences emotions exactly the same way a baby does. One part of your ego would therefore still like someone to lean over you and smile at you – just as happened in your crib back then. Only then can your NES experience feelings of joy. This means that you always need someone else to first show their feelings before you can experience those same feelings. And it also results in a particular quirk that is a primary component of your highly sensitive being.

Accordingly, your NES wants to get others to react emotionally (for instance, as a reaction to your outstanding performance).

You want to elicit emotions in others.

This principle is true across the entire range of possible emotions. There are some HSPs who take a ghoulish delight in provoking other people, just to trigger an emotional reaction. In doing so, they not only discover whether or not the other person represents a danger (the NES's need for security), but they can also absorb the emotional outbursts of others. By doing this, they hope to more fully activate their own somewhat underdeveloped emotional lives. They begin to become more aware of their own feelings. There are actually some HSPs who, because of this, constantly do things that drive the people around them crazy – just to be able to experience their emotional outbursts.

However, this also works wonderfully in a more positive sense. For example, take the feeling of gratitude. If you are a typical HSP, you love this emotion. You will always be attempting to elicit this feeling in others, simply so that, as a result, you can feel positive about yourself.

This trait can also be exploited, however. All anyone would need to do would be to simply not react to you. You would then keep pushing until you have elicited at least some kind of emotional reaction from the other person. If the person in question is especially high up on your list, you won't let up until you have finally attained that which is so vital to your emotional survival.

Incidentally, this is also what happens to many HSPs in unhappy love relationships. Should the traumatic situation arise where the object of their affection doesn't react to them or doesn't do so sufficiently (gives them the cold shoulder), then you will see HSPs who turn to self-destructive behavior just to try to provoke some sort of declaration of love from the other person. Their tremendous mental powers lead to this battle for survival being literally burned into their brains. With their enormous mental intensity, they then forcefully and irrevocably link their neuronal synapses. The great love of their lives is forever seared firmly into their minds (for more about this, read my book *Empaths Love Differently*).

If, on the other hand, the object of affection had declared their love on a daily basis, it would never have come to this. Quite the contrary: The HSP would have quickly become bored, and it would never have led to such a dramatic scene – even though it was the very same person.

Many people ultimately learn that the biggest dramas in their love lives were never actually about the other person, but simply the failed attempt to absorb certain emotions through that person. It was actually all the result of the NES's insatiable need for the emotions of others.

Sometimes, to experience more joy in life yourself, you first need to experience the positive reactions of other people.

This is also the main reason that so many HSPs have careers related to social work. Here, they find it especially easy to meet their own basic emotional needs. In helping others, they are actually generating friendly feelings in the other people. This brings them great joy and a sense of purpose. It also fits in well with their strong ethical values. Last but not least, it also allows them to live out their subtle inborn claim to leadership.

Unfortunately, however, the most unhappy HSPs are frequently found working in social institutions. Usually, it is the poor working conditions that make them unhappiest. The combination of too much work, too little time, and, added to that, the ingratitude of their superiors drives many HSPs to despair.

Still, the philosophy behind helping people is virtually a perfect fit for you. This doesn't mean, however, that you necessarily have to work in a position where you are directly providing help. Basically, any job that allows you to provoke positive feelings in other people will also be good for you. So, if you want to enjoy your job more, the work that you perform needs to touch others emotionally.

All of this leads clearly to the first criterion of your vocational calling: You want your work to touch others emotionally so that you will then be able to vicariously experience those positive feelings.

1. You would like to IMPROVE or ENRICH other people's lives.

Indeed, this gives you a deep sense of purpose. Unfortunately, there are also many people who forget themselves in the process. As time goes on, they develop a kind of "helper syndrome." Some go so far as to sacrifice themselves just to be able to experience more gratitude. This, incidentally, is the very definition of martyrdom.

Making things all the more difficult is the fact that HSPs always have an exaggerated sense of duty. I've already referred to this latent masochistic tendency several times. This nearly always leads to burnout and self-destructive behavior.

Still, your HES is always looking out for you. If you were following your true vocational calling, it would be impossible for you to behave in a self-destructive way. So apparently your calling cannot solely consist of wanting to IMPROVE or ENRICH the lives of others.

Your true vocational calling must therefore include something else, something that protects you from the helper syndrome. A kind of firewall that will protect you from overstretching your desire to help. For a more thorough description of your vocation, a second factor must now enter the picture.

4.2 SELF-ESTEEM

You've just learned that your NES can only be trained to adequately express emotions when other people respond to you with positive feelings. This is the only way you can experience feelings of purpose and happiness – in other words, to enjoy your work.

There is a catch, however. This trait clashes with your strong desire to be ACKNOWLEDGED. You could quickly find yourself in situations where you are in danger of abandoning your own needs and ignoring the boundaries you have set. You would then become a victim of your own design.

In your desire to experience the positive feelings brought on by gratitude, you might just forget that little word called "*no*." Especially if you work for a company, it will then be like you are stuck in a hamster wheel, running your legs off, just to get your clients, co-workers., managers, etc. to express their gratitude.

What you need is to develop an inner sense of self-protectiveness. The goal should be for this to allow you to continue to ENRICH or IMPROVE the lives of others while at the same time helping you observe the boundaries you've established to protect you from becoming overwhelmed.

You need to supplement your attempts to elicit positive emotional feedback with a sense of self-esteem.

Not until you develop a sufficient sense of self-esteem will you stop overtaxing yourself and negatively over-reacting to feelings of not being appreciated. Only by loving yourself more will you be able to protect yourself from yourself.

I can already hear your objections – *easier said than done,* you will say – and you will once again be more than right. For decades, generations of psychologists and psychiatrists have been gnashing their teeth over precisely this problem.

It's not as though you can simply tell yourself every morning that, as of today, you are going to love and respect yourself more. You are far too intelligent for this silly little game to work. You can use positive thinking or other autosuggestion techniques until you are blue in the face. For intuitive people, it's far too easy to see through these attempts at self-deception for them to be effective.

But you don't even need these kinds of psychological strategies. I have become firmly convinced that HSPs are practically predestined to take a different path to developing more self-esteem. You simply have to give yourself an extremely specific reason:

If you want to be proud of yourself, you need to do something you can be proud of.

You will likely never be able to completely lose your performance mindset. This means that there is just one single situation in which you will be able to be happy with yourself: when you DEVELOP (invent) something that comes exclusively from your own efforts – when you are, so to speak, the inventor. When you create something of your own, something for which only you are responsible. This is the thing that will allow you to feel proud of yourself.

You will create moments in which you are actually grateful to yourself. From this point on, you will begin to be able to generate feelings of gratitude on your own. You will no longer exclusively have to depend on *other people* reacting positively to you.

And so, the circle closes. Remember, slumbering within you is a tremendous resource: your CREATIVE POWERS. It has surely now quickly become clear why you possess this fantastic gift. Your inventiveness, your creativity, and your intuition are as strong as they are for a very specific reason: These gifts are just what you will need to CREATE precisely that which allows you to be proud of yourself.

Now, you probably also realize just why you are a "mediator" between the VISIBLE and INVISIBLE WORLDS. After all, as an HSP, only you have the ability to think up something brand new that will also be beneficial to you and your fellow human beings. This will give a major boost to your self-esteem. You are no longer following along with the ideas of others. You are not simply a cog in some massive production process. Now, you are the one who is coming up with the ideas.

This is actually the second main aspect of your vocational calling. It means that not only do you want to ENRICH and IMPROVE the lives of others, but you also want to create the means to do so.

2. You not only want to improve and enrich other people's lives, but you also want to create a PROJECT OF YOUR OWN to do so.

The pieces of the bigger picture are beginning to fit together. More and more, the myriad little mosaic stones of your complex being are coming together to create an image of a specific vocation. It would have been utterly contradictory to your destiny to have given you a powerful HES, but at the same time to have endowed you with a personality that allowed you to receive love and recognition without having to do anything to earn it. This combination of personality traits would be completely illogical because you would never be able to develop any inner incentive to recognize your own creativity and put it into action. You would lapse into laziness and self-indulgence. Any drive to accomplish something with your life would literally be nipped in the bud.

Now you can understand why, in the past, you always had the feeling that something was missing in your life. And you would have been right, since feeling a certain inner emptiness is always a sign that there is something you need to do. This inner void now needs to be FILLED. Everything in your personality was designed from the start for this. This is what will lead to vocational fulFILLMENT:

You possess a performance mindset because you do, indeed, want to accomplish something – just within the framework of a project of your own.

So, forgive the fates for this little (and perhaps unfair) trick. Everything in you is targeted toward your desire to actually CREATE something of YOUR OWN, something that will also allow you to take pride in yourself. This will provide you with not only your urgently needed sense of self-esteem, but also an all-round feeling of satisfaction with yourself. Your "inner glow" will become outwardly apparent, giving you the external aura you have always longed for. Your emotional transformation will be obvious to others. Then, all you need to do to be more visible is to simply be present. You will realize that it had never been necessary for you to be more assertive or a better actor. Now that you have created something of your own, you will observe something happening externally:

People respect you because you respect yourself.

You will still enjoy being able to IMPROVE or ENRICH the lives of others, but you will no longer fall into the trap of self-sacrifice. You are now emotionally stable enough to be able to utter an inconvenient "*no.*" You have massively reduced your dependency on positive feedback. Even if someone is offended – or even becomes aggressive – you will not lose your sense of self-esteem. As of now, when things get to be too much, you will say "*stop!*" People who like themselves also protect themselves.

4.3 VARIETY

At this point, the danger of getting caught up in helper syndrome or of pursuing overblown attempts to gain acknowledgement will finally have been averted. Still, nothing will have changed the fact that you take the most pleasure in your work when you can use your OWN PROJECT to IMPROVE or ENRICH the lives of those around you. This is simply a wonderful reflection of your highly sensitive core nature.

Doing good in the world, supporting others, making others happy, and, as a result of this, also experiencing positive emotional reactions yourself, will always give you a strong sense of purpose.

It is simply the nature of things that when our environment always remains the same, it's not possible to guarantee that positive reactions will constantly be generated. Sooner or later, everything will just become habitual and taken for granted. You will then find yourself having to constantly go to extremes to satisfy your hunger for emotional reactions. This would certainly not only *not* be in your best interest, but it would also ignite a renewed risk of you overburdening yourself.

> You want to experience the emotions of a VARIETY of people every day.

This would also seem to be a contradiction to your highly sensitive personality. On one hand, you love solitude and therefore have to be careful not to overwhelm yourself with too many external stimuli. On the other hand, your emotional realm needs feedback from other people.

If we take a closer look, though, this is not a contradiction at all. It's just related to the different stages of your PERSONAL GROWTH. Once you have finally LET GO and found peace, you will notice at some point that the longer you close yourself off mentally, emotionally, or physically, the worse your mood becomes.

Some HSPs attempt to solve this problem by using their families or partners to compensate for the fact that they have shut themselves off from the rest of the world. They quickly become aware, however, that this places too large a burden on their loved ones at home. It's just not reasonable to expect partners, relatives, and especially our own children to constantly provide us with positive emotional reactions.

What you need to do is to strike the utmost balance between shutting yourself off from the world and being fully engaged with it. Especially in your professional life, this would virtually be a win-win situation. In your private life, you could still live as the natural introvert you are, while in public, you could fulfill your (urgent) need for the emotional reactions of other people.

Especially when it comes to your job, it would also be ideal if other people were automatically required to focus on you. Face-to-face conversations, for instance, would be great for you. Every personal customer consultation or sales talk would cater to your desire to experience the diversity of human reactions.

However, leading a seminar or other group event, as long as it fell under the proper low-stress conditions, would also be something well-suited to you. Teaching jobs can also fulfill these requirements. Your higher position of authority in relation to the group could also allow you to enjoy a certain degree of protection.

All in all, it's not surprising, that many HSPs find work as consultants, salespersons, or seminar leaders. Putting yourself in the spotlight guarantees that others will at least always notice you and automatically react to you.

This leaves us with the people who work in artistic fields, seeking to experience the emotional reactions of their audiences. This kind of situation is also very popular with HSPs. Being able to touch others emotionally through their work allows them to experience an indirect focus on themselves. The same is true for design engineers who are delighted when customers react positively to their inventions, just as it is for highly sensitive hotel managers who find enjoyment in their work through the satisfaction and gratitude of their guests.

Jobs that involve contact with customers, audiences, visitors, guests, listeners, readers, or other consumers essentially provide the perfect setting for you to experience the degree of emotional variety you crave. This would also imply, however, that jobs that involve B2B (business-to-business) contact would not be well-suited for you. Communications from company to company are too full of dry, business-related aspects to be able provide you with sufficient emotional – and above all, positive – feedback.

Of course, you may also be thinking that you could find a way to fulfill your need for emotional reactions in your private life, rather than at work. I can only tell you that, in my experience, this strategy works in only the rarest of cases.

If you were to attempt to make up for a lack of enjoyment on the job through specific recreational pastimes, you would, unfortunately, hopelessly overburden yourself. First, you would then be spending the majority of your life in a work situation that doesn't correspond to your vocational calling. And second, you would unavoidably place yourself under an excessive amount of stress in your private life. This means that you would no longer be able to use your free time to relax or pursue other interests (or for your love life) and, on top of that, not only would you need to be receiving positive emotional feedback from the people in your private life, but you would also need that group of people to be constantly changing.

Unfortunately, people with a highly sensitive nature are not very well suited for spending their free time constantly trying to meet new people or conjure up new acquaintances. Not to mention the massive effort it would require if you had to use private resources to draw attention to yourself so that, in the end, you could hopefully experience a fountain of gratitude or other positive emotions. Trying to do all this alongside your job would be a gargantuan effort. Usually, teenagers or young adults are the only people who can cope with this level of stress in their private lives.

Sooner or later, HSPs who attempt to have their emotional needs fulfilled exclusively in their private lives will fail. They are setting themselves up for disappointment. And at some point, this profusion of disappointment is going to mutate into a negative view of the world. Some HSPs even come to the conclusion that people are evil, cruel, and ungrateful. They don't stop to consider that they have simply tried to positively stimulate their emotional lives in a way that was completely ill-suited to their highly sensitive nature.

In summary, it will be significantly easier for you to come into contact with a variety of different people in the context of professional activities or those with no particular emotional component. This would allow you to spend all of your free time pursuing other interests or simply enjoying pleasant, undisturbed downtime. This would create a *work-life-balance* that would be nearly perfect for an HSP.

And this leads us to the third important criterion for your vocation:

> 3. You want to develop your own project – one that will improve and enrich the lives of CUSTOMERS, VISITORS, and GUESTS.

Your professional target group will therefore be private consumers and not B2B clients.

For the sake of completeness, I would like to also mention that another important reason exists for your need for so much variety in your life. It is your intuition, which wants to be put to use. Every day, it provides you with ideas, creativity, and knowledge that it wants to see put into practice. This latent potential wants to rise to the surface: Inventors want to invent, designers want to design, and creatives want to create.

This is why, for instance, you will encounter HSPs in the development units of corporations or in university laboratories, or in other places where creativity and inventiveness are called for, who practically jump for joy at the launch of another new project or when the focus is on novelty itself.

So, it doesn't necessarily need to be the emotions of different people (which, however, would be ideal for your NES) that provide you with enjoyment on the job, but even just variety, in and of itself, would be more than sufficient.

Incidentally, there is even a specific technical term that has been given to this longing for variety. *Dr. Elaine Aron*, the American psychologist and sole inventor of the term "high sensitivity" coined the term *high sensation seeking*. She, too, was able to observe that at a certain stage in their PERSONAL GROWTH, the tendency of HSPs to be reclusive is supplemented by a desire for variety and adventure. After reading this sub-chapter, it should now be clear to you why this expression of *Elaine Aron's* is absolutely fitting.

We now come to the final criterion for your vocational calling. Once you learn about this, you will understand the reason that, all your life, you have been asking *why*.

4.4 UNDERSTANDING

If you think back to the beginning of this book, you will remember that I claimed that you had always been preoccupied with the *whys* in life. This trait is ingrained in you because, quite simply, you will need it in your vocation. It is the final little piece of the mosaic – now, the overall picture of your vocational calling will slowly come into view.

To repeat: It is impossible for you to fulfill all of your highly sensitive needs exclusively in your private life. You need your free time to pursue other interests, for recreation, for your love life, and, above all, to disengage for a while. To avoid creating an overwhelming double burden for yourself, you are instead virtually compelled to satisfy your need for the emotional reactions of your fellow human beings within your professional sphere.

The problem with this is that you no longer possess a cute little baby face that people automatically react to with kindness and happiness. What you really need above all is something that triggers the same reaction in people as a baby's smile. You need some kind of alternative, something else that will cause people to react the way you want them to while, at the same time, allowing the whole thing to point back to you. You can achieve this by CREATING SOMETHING OF YOUR OWN. You will then automatically be seen the originator or the inventor, and all of the emotional reactions will reflect back on you.

Now you just have to figure out what it might be that could substitute for that baby face you no longer possess. The solution would be for you to develop specific products or services. These could then take the place of you personally in IMPROVING and ENHANCING the lives of others. You wouldn't even have to be present in person to make other people happy. You would simply allow your products or services to do this so that you yourself could remain in the background (which would surely be your preference).

The whole concept would also fit in perfectly with the fact that you wanted to work with CUSTOMERS, GUESTS, VISITORS, or other END USERS anyway, so that you could experience more emotional variety. And, since you would also like to strengthen your sense of self-esteem and therefore want to create your OWN PROJECT, as a part of that, you could also act as an INVENTOR in developing particular products or services.

In the end, you would have created a substitute for your baby face. You would have enjoyed enough variety, you would have created something of your own, and you will ultimately be the recipient of gratitude for this.

If you go back and look again at everything that has been said so far, you will see that all of your abilities and talents are targeted to very specific professional activities:

You want to create your OWN PROJECT in which you develop PRODUCTS AND SERVICES that IMPROVE and ENRICH the lives of others.

Incidentally, this is still nothing out of the ordinary. An enormous number of professionals or company owners also harbor the same desire. And yet, not everyone is cut out to succeed at this. There is a very specific challenge that must be conquered. You must first figure out exactly what it is that makes people feel grateful. And this is precisely the point where we come to all of your *why* questions. These questions are not about trying to better understand *yourself* – they are about something else entirely:

It's not yourself that you want to understand better – it's others!

This means that there is a high likelihood that what is behind your love of brooding about things is merely a misunderstanding. You don't really want to rack your brains over the world, or your life, or even over yourself. It's more the case that the reason you possess so many talents is because you are actually interested in entirely different questions:

- Why do certain products or services make people feel happy while others don't?
- Why do customers, audiences, visitors, guests, or other consumers view something as an improvement or enrichment of their lives?
- Why do they view other things as not improving or enriching their lives?
- Why are customers, audiences, visitors, guests, or other consumers prepared to spend money on one thing and not on another?

All of your highly sensitive traits are precisely targeted to finding the optimal answers to exactly these types of questions.

Only you are able to rely on extremely fine-tuned powers of intuition and observation to do so. This makes you, as an HSP, optimally suited to recognize, with pin-point accuracy, the needs and wishes of other people. You are the ideal service provider.

On top of that, you also possess the necessary CREATIVE POWER to be able to DEVELOP exactly what consumers desire. You are practically predestined to be able to understand CUSTOMERS, AUDIENCES, VISITORS, GUESTS, and OTHER CONSUMERS. Only you would be capable of being a true master of this.

You possess an abundance of enviable gifts that allow to you to recognize with pin-point accuracy what others desire – and what they don't.

The majority of company owners who go bankrupt do so because they don't possess precisely these abilities. They don't comprehend the true needs of other people because they just don't possess sufficient intuition. Usually, they have developed their products or services without taking people's actual desires into account, and then have to invest in expensive advertising campaigns to artificially create a need where there wasn't one. This only succeeds in the rarest of cases. These types of executives simply don't have any entrepreneurial talent. You, on the other hand, do!

Your powerful intuition also means that you have entrepreneurial talent.

Now you may understand why you never got ahead when you were spending your time trying to understand yourself. And you surely also now know why you only came up with fantastic solutions and tips when it was about other people's needs and desires. You would seldom have been able to come up with such satisfactory solutions for your own wants and need. This trait is known as "service-orientation" or "customer-orientation."

Your entire nature is designed exclusively to allow you to understand others. If you emphasize putting this talent to work in your professional life, it will more than pay off. And with that, we have discovered the fourth criterion for your vocational calling:

4. You want to UNDERSTAND the needs of consumers.

This is also the reason why the most successful products and services have generally been (and still will be) developed by highly sensitive people.

4.5 PUTTING IT ALL TOGETHER

You take pleasure in your work when the following criteria can be fulfilled through your professional activities:

1. It makes you feel good when you IMPROVE or ENRICH the lives of others.
2. You want to DEVELOP SOMETHING OF YOUR OWN that you can take pride in, so that you can replace your striving to be ACKNOWLEDGED with feelings of self-esteem.
3. You want your work to appeal to a great number of different people so that you can experience NEW EMOTIONAL REACTIONS every day.
4. You attempt to UNDERSTAND PEOPLE and why they view one thing as an improvement to their lives and another thing as not.

From here on out, I am going to be very careful about citing specific examples, because ultimately, it isn't about finding a quantitative definition of your vocation, but rather, a qualitative one.

It's never about narrowing things down to one particular profession or one specific industry. It's much more about the working conditions you need and the way you want to be able to carry out your responsibilities. There are many areas of the business world that can fulfill these parameters, which also explains why you can find HSPs in nearly every sector of industry.

I also don't want to inject any (foreign) concepts into your life that aren't your own. This is why I kept the discussion above quite general. I will, however, provide one specific example, so that you can at least better comprehend the underlying principle.

If, in our example, you were to paint a picture, then this would be a way for you to ENRICH or IMPROVE the life of someone else a bit (if they were to hang it in their living room). This would have allowed you to serve as a mediator for non-HSPs between the invisible world (ideas, creativity, sense of harmony) and the visible world. On top of that, you probably would be the recipient of gratitude, expressed in the form of words or payment. This would do you a world of good.

What's more, you would have been involved in the complete product creation cycle. From the initial idea to the production itself to the ultimate sale. This always generates a sense of purpose. And, you would have DEVELOPED something brand new – making you the sole inventor of the picture. You would have made full use of your CREATIVE POWERS. This is precisely what makes you feel proud – you would have CREATED SOMETHING OF YOUR OWN, something connected only with you, yourself. This would also be very satisfying to you.

In this example, however, something specific is missing. This would only fulfill the first two items in my definition of your vocational calling. The third and fourth criteria still haven't been taken into account. Your picture would now be gone, and you would be receiving NO ADDITIONAL GRATITUDE for it. You also wouldn't have put to use your exceptional talent for UNDERSTANDING. You probably would have just randomly painted anything that occurred to you.

Painting pictures, in and of itself, therefore, can't be considered a potential vocation for your highly sensitive self. It could, however, be a nice way to relax. Beyond that, it could also be a way for you to train your creativity – in other words, your connection to the invisible world. Drawing and painting are also wonderfully well-suited as forms of meditation. Unfortunately, however, this still has very little to do with your vocational calling.

But we can still take our example of your self-created painting and adapt it to fit. We just need to incorporate the other two criteria (VARIETY and UNDERSTANDING). To do this, you wouldn't be allowed to just sell your painting to one individual customer. You would have to create an art print of it. This would allow you to bring pleasure to many more people. You would have developed just one single product, but it could be enjoyed by many different people all at the same time. This would allow you to experience many more emotional reactions from within your environment without the pressure of having to constantly create something new. And you would be able to fulfill at least the third parameter for sustained enjoyment on the job: VARIETY.

We're just missing the fourth criterion (UNDERSTANDING). You could fulfill this condition by not painting any picture at all at first. Instead, the first step would be to investigate which art prints were most in demand in the industry. This would allow you to employ your great talent for UNDERSTANDING, because to do this, you will have to speak to as many manufacturers or experts as possible. Since you are an HSP, you alone will have been able to figure everything out after this. Only you possess the intuition and powers of observation needed to develop a sixth sense for the right thing. In contrast to non-HSPs, you can judge with a high degree of accuracy which pictures or kinds of pictures are going to be in demand. And only after this would you begin to paint. So, you wouldn't have painted something from your own imagination, but rather, something that would attract potential buyers for your artwork. By fulfilling this fourth aspect, you would then have satisfied all four criteria for your vocational calling.

Taking all of this into account, you can now clearly see the definition of your vocational calling. You were born for one reason alone:

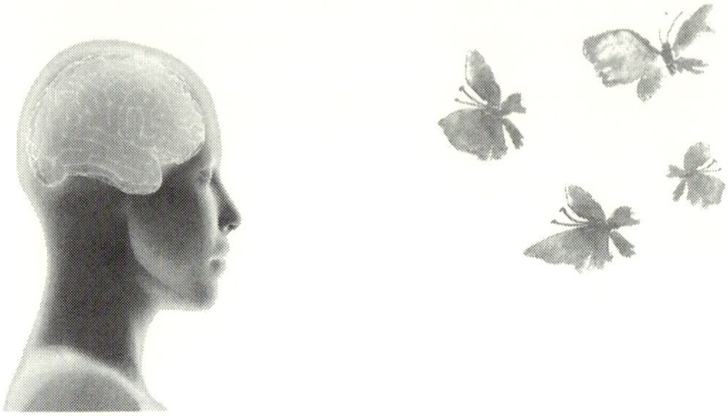

Your calling is to develop products or services that improve or enrich the lives of those who use them.

You now know, at least in theory, what your vocational calling is. You just need to determine how to find it in concrete terms. So, let's turn our attention to the final supreme discipline of your highly sensitive life path, so that you will be able to then track down your own personal vocational calling.

5 How Do I Find My Vocational Calling?

As you now know, in your vocation, your focus is fundamentally going to be not on yourself but on the people around you. Sooner or later, you will see that this is a basic life principle to which you are clearly subject. If, contrary to this, you were to put your AES at the center of things (*I'll paint the kind of pictures I want to paint*), it may be possible for you to create a fulfilling hobby for yourself, but you will never have the sense that you are following your vocational calling.

> If you UNDERSTAND how others look at things, you will no longer have to worry about your own future.

To this day, I still haven't found any reasonable explanation for this phenomenon. But nearly every HSP who has found their way to a fulfilling professional life has repeatedly confirmed this statement. Only *after* they have made the interests of others (customers, guests, visitors, etc.) the top priority in their jobs have their own desires consequently been fulfilled.

This would also explain, incidentally, why HSPs rarely make any money with questionable business tactics, tricks, or shortcuts (for instance, making a quick profit on the stock market). In these types of situations, the fates are even aligned against those involved.

In short, when you take an interest in the egos of others, you will capitalize on this. If, on the other hand, you proceed on the basis of your own egocentric perspective, this will likely result in a life filled with financial ups and downs.

When you IMPROVE or ENRICH the lives of others, you will also IMPROVE and ENRICH your own life.

All in all, however, it will become increasingly clear to you that a traditional employment arrangement is fairly at odds with your vocational calling. Nonetheless, I have met some HSPs who were still able to follow their calling even under such conditions. Most of them work for companies, associations, organizations, public institutions, or other employers where they are given the opportunity to work fully independently to DEVELOP NEW PRODUCTS OR SERVICES THAT OTHER PEOPLE (customers, guests, visitors, etc.) CAN ENJOY. In these cases, the HSPs were actually given an opportunity to pursue their vocational calling within the framework of a traditional employment situation.

Unfortunately, it is becoming increasingly rare to find these kinds of conditions in today's working world. The alternative would, in fact, be to start up a small business yourself (or to completely take over or become a partner in an existing one). As the owner, you would also have employees, which is an important factor for you. These employees could relieve you of all of those tasks you were never destined to do. In addition, you would have the ability to divide up your time the way you like as well as develop a great sense of SELF-ESTEEM because you have DEVELOPED your own company. Not to mention your subtle inborn CLAIM TO LEADERSHIP, which you'll certainly also be able to put into practice.

You are the idea generator and guide for the people who work for you and put your plans into action.

This means that as a self-employed HSP, only when you are in a position to limit your activities exclusively to management, development, and strategy-related tasks and delegate everything else will you have the success you have always longed for. As the employ*er*, you need to assign work to your employ*ees*. Rather than slaving away, take on the tasks of guiding, inventing, planning, and evaluating, and assume ultimate responsibility.

Never forget that an innate entrepreneurial talent lies dormant deep within you. It will never be able to make itself known if, even though you are self-employed, you cram your working days full of tasks that need to be carried out. Only you, as an HSP, have the ability to truly UNDERSTAND the needs of your customers. And, you also have the proper UNDERSTANDING OF HARMONIOUSNESS to know what fits into the world and what doesn't. Thanks to your (now functional) INTUITION, you KNOW exactly whether a product, a particular service, or a new strategy has the potential to succeed.

Taken all together, this means that you therefore have a choice: You can attempt to create a situation where, although you work for someone else, your working conditions are similar to those of being self-employed, or you can start up, buy up, or become a partner in a company. I know very well that you can't simply snap your fingers and start up or restructure a small company (and it certainly isn't going to happen overnight), so don't get ahead of yourself in your thoughts about starting up a business (or hiring employees).

Still, once you have finished reading this book, you will find the same question popping up again and again in your mind: *Should I branch out on my own now or not?* My only response to this is that you should not do anything at all for right now. I know that for many of you, this advice is very unsatisfying, but it is precisely the right answer. There is a simple explanation for this:

First, there is no universal recommendation that I could make here. Your situation is so specific to your own life that there is no way for me to be able to provide you with professional guidance long-distance. Second, when the time is right, you will no longer need any tips from me, since you yourself will then possess the necessary KNOWLEDGE. You are the one who is going to possess a breathtakingly powerful intuition (even if the fire in your brain is not yet quite out).

If you are still experiencing some vague problems or even apparently irresolvable conflicts for which you simply can't find answers or solutions, this is always a helpful gauge in identifying how far along you are in your PERSONAL GROWTH and whether you're already moving into an INTUITIVELY LED LIFE.

If you find you don't know what to do,
you haven't yet fully put the aspect of
LETTING GO into practice.

It is then high time to focus more fully on the present instead of spending time contemplating plans for the future. Rather than putting the idea of starting up a company on your agenda, the only thing you should do is to return to the advice in Chapter 3: "What Do I Need to Do to Let Go?"

Only by LETTING GO will you allow your
enormous intuitive abilities to fully unfold.

Only once you are sufficiently *grounded* will you be able to start living an INTUITIVELY LED LIFE. Even if it sounds paradoxical, everything you need for this already exists. You just have to look at it the right way. Based on experience, right at this very moment, you yourself, your surroundings, and the people around you are providing you with everything that you need. You probably simply need to let go of certain ideas about life that didn't originate within you so that the ideas that do truly come from within you can appear before your eyes. Whenever you have absolutely no idea what you should do (and are perhaps even feeling a sense of desperation), it is better to stop fighting against what life is handing you and do battle with your own hard-headedness instead. What doesn't work – doesn't work! And what works – works!

Become a master at recognizing which doors are open and leaving those that are closed shut.

I know well from my own experience that it can take a long time to break free of some of the chains of the past. Sometimes, even years. This is also part of the nature of things. In addition to their vocational calling, HSPs, in particular, have yet another, higher-level life challenge to master.

I have become convinced that, for you, the most important issue is ultimately to establish INTRINSIC TRUST. This is obvious, though – after all, you possess a NEWBORN EGO STATE that is permanently battling saber-toothed tigers and woolly mammoths. Your NES is plagued by PRIMAL FEARS. This means that you begin your existence on this earth at the opposite end of the spectrum from self-confidence. And this makes you further removed than anyone else from your ultimate life goal – developing INTRINSIC TRUST. Once again, there is something you are going to need to DEVELOP (this is probably starting to sound familiar by now).

For HSPs, their ultimate purpose in life is to develop INTRINSIC TRUST.

You therefore need to be aware of something important about your life. There is a difference between your calling and your life purpose:

- Your CALLING is that which you can do.
- Your PURPOSE is that which you must do.

You could also say that your calling is that which you have the ability to do. That for which you have a talent. The need for PERSONAL GROWTH, however, is something that you *absolutely* must accomplish for you to even begin to live a life that fills you with satisfaction – especially outside of your professional activities.

Making it your life's mission to rid yourself of your PRIMAL FEARS is definitely not a piece of cake. You are not going to be able to master this challenging aspect of your PERSONAL GROWTH overnight. It will probably take you most of your life to be able to conquer all of your PRIMAL FEARS. Developing INTRINSIC TRUST can also be a very drawn-out process. It is in the nature of things that this leads to the emergence of different phases of life. And this, of course, has an influence on your search for your vocational calling. The sooner you determine your PURPOSE in life, the sooner you will also – in the process – discover your CALLING.

It is notable, however, that many HSPs find this process of learning to be courageous and overcome hurdles to be extremely difficult. They often report illnesses, personal drama, major upheavals, or other blows of fate. It may be that these unpleasant circumstances only arise because some HSPs stubbornly refuse to accept their purpose in life – to dare to trust themselves more than they ever have before. Who knows ...?

It is, however, also conceivable that all of this simply is part of what it means to be a highly sensitive person. Even in ancient historical narratives or in certain biographies, we repeatedly see people whose lives are full of conflict. This often involves people who are considered to be spiritual leaders, who are described as selfless helpers who, with their guidance and wisdom, attained brilliance. They themselves, in contrast, were plagued by a lack of stability in their lives and severe inner doubts. This then leads people to speak of the path of martyrs or crusaders. A deep spiritual conflict with life that, at the end, however, is marked by salvation.

Even in the biographies of geniuses who have bequeathed to humanity masterworks of art, literature, or science, the same themes appear over and over again: their arduous journeys to mastering life itself without succumbing to depression or bitterness.

Now you can surely better understand why I was literally compelled to include such an extensive chapter on the topic of LETTING GO in this book. It was to help you protect yourself from this kind of personal drama and to do better than the great masters. Moreover, please don't think that you are condemned to only creating something earth-shattering. It is far more likely that you are meant to do something else entirely.

There are millions and millions of highly sensitive people in the world who are far more likely to quietly and unobtrusively have a positive influence on their surroundings. Their spiritual influence on humanity generally takes place out of the public eye. I therefore believe that it is largely in smaller ways that HSPs play out their important role in society – that they perhaps even function as a kind of spiritual counselor or guardian angel. They often have a greater influence on other people's lives than they themselves are even aware of. The other person benefits from their words or actions, while the HSP has no idea that they have just performed a valuable service.

If, however, HSPS were to play a determining role in the lives of those around them, this would also mean that they themselves must also be part of a pre-determined destiny. And this would bring us back to the topic of life purpose. Something would have to be at work that had a far greater influence on the lives of highly sensitive people than of non-highly sensitive people.

The lives of HSPs are probably more highly influenced by fate than by free will.

This is true, at least, until you have developed sufficient INTRINSIC TRUST. This means that not until you have LIBERATED yourself (for instance, from concepts about life that were never your own) and established enough INTRINSIC TRUST will you be free. And then whatever has been determined by fate can be replaced by free will. From that point on, you will have the ability to manage your life on your own, in the way that you choose.

Until then, however, you will probably still be affected by your own intuition's "emergency response measures." This means that, to help build up INTRINSIC TRUST, your own body is going to let you know when you have gotten too far away from your life goal. Then, your HES is going to intervene and make course corrections, whether or not your AES – in other words, you, yourself – is pleased with this.

HSPs with some life experience, who can look back over decades of their lives, are especially likely to confirm this over and over again. In retrospect, they can see where certain life dramas actually were necessary. At the time of the crisis, however, it would have always been difficult for them to recognize the greater purpose behind it. Only after many years had passed were they able to discover the common thread. Ultimately, they came to realize that without the suffering they had endured, they never would have evolved in their PERSONAL GROWTH to the extent that they had. Only after the fact did they realize that they had continually been making use of a wonderful natural law:

When one door closes,
another one always opens.

Just as in this lovely old poem from an unknown poet:

Whenever you think you can't go on,
From somewhere, a light begins to dawn,

It comes to you, an encouraging sign,
Inspiring in you songs divine.

How easy to bear life's vicissitudes,
with your courage and faith
once more renewed.

This unpleasant alternation between suffering (the door closes) and RESOLUTION (a new door opens) is similar to the confrontation therapy or desensitization therapy used in classical psychology. For HSPs, however, it is not a psychologist who guides them, but rather their HIGHER EGO STATE – in other words, their own intuition.

Fateful life crises, however, also fulfill an important function in your life by allowing you to increase your resilience (mental resistance). If you experience first-hand that for every problem, no matter how daunting, there is ultimately always a satisfactory solution, at some point, you will realize that you never need to worry again. You will have gained the certainty that, without exception, your intuition will lead you to the next open door so that you can confidently step through it. This deep certainty that there will always be a (positive) solution is what we then refer to as INTRINSIC TRUST – the belief in your own intuition. In this case, any suffering that took place beforehand would have actually only been a therapeutic strategy chosen by your own body.

To help you better assess which stage you are at in the development of INTRINSIC TRUST, I now want to cover the individual phases of PERSONAL GROWTH. They are categorized as follows:

1. The Intellectualization Phase
2. The Overload Phase
3. The Life-Negating Phase
4. The Awakening Phase
5. The Liberation Phase

Incidentally, repeating or skipping some of the individual phases is completely normal. There are also still additional life phases, but I will not be discussing these other phases. First, because a discussion of these topics would go beyond the scope of this book and second, because it simply is unnecessary. *The Vocational Calling for Highly Sensitive Persons* starts at a much earlier point than would require addressing these other later phases. I go into these in one of my other books, *Empaths Love Differently*, which deals primarily with self-love and intrinsic trust.

Let's get started with the first phase.

5.1 THE INTELLECTUALIZATION PHASE

This first phase is where all HSPs begin their adult lives. I also often refer to it as the phase of naïveté.

Your NES is effectively still your unsolved problem, and your brain is not yet fully tuned into your HES. You can sense that you have a distinct potential for intuitive powers, and you routinely experience strange coincidences or other mysterious events, but at this stage, you can't yet put all of the pieces together. What you have become aware of early on, however, is your strong conscience, your need for things to be harmonious, and your idealized notions of freedom, justice, and truth.

All in all, however, at this phase, with this combination of your evident personal traits, there isn't much you can do. You still believe that there is something wrong with you, something wrong with the world, and that you have somehow ended up on the wrong planet. This results in a subtle feeling of insecurity. You build up an enormous emotional protective wall around yourself. Your emotions ultimately atrophy or become characterized by extremes (boundless joy, hopeless depression). You could say that you're not completely rooted in reality. You are deeply ENTANGLED in your many PRIMAL FEARS. Your intellect begins to take on an exaggerated role. Your AES starts to take on tasks nature never intended it to.

In this phase, you believe that your mind is the only true measure of all things.

You are now being too cerebral. Every day, countless ideas bounce through your head as to all the different careers you could pursue. But since you are largely untethered from reality, you are simply left hanging in the air. You are not grounded. Your intuition isn't functioning properly, meaning you are not capable of generating CONCRETE KNOWLEDGE about what you want or don't want.

Instead, you look to your parents, relatives, friends or partner. You also allow the internet, television, films, or books to plant desires in you that are not your own. You are helpless in the face of these countless temptations. Every day, you take on ideas and desires that have come from outside yourself, which are most likely in direct opposition to your highly sensitive nature. You replace your own inner truths with other people's truths. You fall into a kind of hypnosis from which you will only AWAKEN years later. These are the common types of threats that HSPs, in particular, are exposed to at the beginning of their lives.

During this phase, it's only natural that you enjoy making use of your mind – after all, you still think it's the only thing that exists. You are delighted at how well it works. In contrast, your emotions seem to you to be very limiting. You share them only with a few select people (if at all). Because you are being tormented (often subconsciously) by vague PRIMAL FEARS, this only affirms your efforts to suppress your emotions. So, you keep your focus on your intellect. This doesn't seem to present any threat. You happily feed your mind with everything imaginable, literally devouring information, opinions, data, and anything else you come across in your desire to expand your knowledge of God and the world.

In your professional life as well, you are one-hundred-percent committed to theory and education. You add on another academic degree, spend a semester abroad, attend yet another seminar.

You would love nothing better than to continue your education for the rest of your life. Once you're finally stuffed full of knowledge and certificates, you may decide to start over again with something new. Many HSPs keep themselves busy learning new professions, completing training to become a certified coach or beginning a new course of study in homeopathic medicine. They are generally open to any sort of continuing education, as long as it allows them to soak up theoretical knowledge like a sponge. It's always better than facing the threat of (emotional) reality.

There are also many HSPs who would actually prefer to do absolutely nothing at all. They find their greatest enjoyment in simply sitting and thinking. Or they lose themselves in daydreams, forever staring off into the distance, or they gaze into the night sky, staring at the stars for hours at a time. They get used to the dangerous game of just letting their thoughts spin around in their heads. They let their mind go wherever it wants to go. And in doing so, they lose themselves in the vast expanse of their INTELLECT.

In this INTELLECTUALIZATION PHASE, HSPs pursue innumerable strategies to avoid having to deal too closely with the sobering reality of life. Whether they do this by amassing theoretical knowledge, doing absolutely nothing, or tucking themselves away, safely ensconced as a little genius in a research lab or an artist in a studio, during this phase, the AES is definitely in charge.

Incidentally, moving beyond this consistently typical initial phase of PERSONAL GROWTH is extremely difficult for HSPs who belong to the inheritance generation or who have delegated the task of earning money to their partners. It's not hard to understand why, since they don't experience a normal, natural confrontation with reality. The act of earning money is perhaps the most natural way to become grounded and make a leap ahead in our PERSONAL GROWTH.

The factors behind this have been ingrained in us since time immemorial. Earning money is a form of hunting, gathering, or harvesting. In earlier times, we hunted woolly mammoths, plucked berries from bushes, or planted our fields. Today, what we hunt, gather, and harvest are slips of paper, but the basic principle remains the same. Earning an income is therefore a primal element of human life. Humans are practically compelled to deal with reality (the present) so that they will ultimately arrive at SOLUTIONS. Thousands of years ago, no one would have even thought of wanting to eat something without having first gone hunting or planting a crop. Anyone who didn't feel like hunting or working in the fields put themselves in danger of either starvation or expulsion from the group, which was equally life-threatening.

This is how at least those HSPs who don't have to work at a job for financial reasons cut themselves off from the natural process of PERSONAL GROWTH. In these cases, the HSPs will have to take their development into their own hands. This self-directed approach, however, is in opposition to the nature of HSPs, who would much rather sit and hope and deny reality than to take action. This leaves them brooding over everything and everyone.

But even those HSPs who were forced to take on a job at a young age face certain risks. Their tendency toward PERFECTIONISM and their PERFORMANCE MINDSET can cause them to quickly run up against a wall in their everyday work. Rather than trying to change their attitude toward their job or simply trading in their current employer for a better one, most of them remain where they are. Instead, they gather even more of a head of steam to make another, harder, dash into that same wall. And then they curse at the world, their employer, or their supervisor. This projection of their own problems onto the rest of the world becomes their daily struggle.

On the other hand, those HSPs who are already self-employed at this stage are not yet able to profit from their ability to UNDERSTAND consumers and markets. Their intuition hasn't yet become accurate enough for them to develop an entrepreneurial sixth sense. They are in danger of pursuing a business concept that is doomed from the start to fail. In their attempts to nonetheless succeed, they will slave away until they collapse from the effort. There is no possibility of achieving inner peace, which means they will also not be able to come up with new solutions, since, ultimately, they have no connection to their own inner guidance. And this results in all kinds of turbulence in their businesses.

To sum it all up, it doesn't matter what kind of professional situation you find yourself in at this stage: More than likely, you are pursuing a path that is ill-suited to you. However, this isn't necessarily a tragic mistake. It could even be that it was predestined. What I mean by this is that all HSPs go through something similar. At this stage, the train has not yet left the station – in this first phase of development for HSPs, there aren't any consequential conflicts. People simply notice that their inner satisfaction and, above all, their enjoyment of life, have become somewhat diminished. This would be the perfect moment to put the ideas in the chapter on LETTING GO into action. That would make the next step, the AWAKENING PHASE, relatively easy to master. And most HSPs do this, too – they become aware of how they have become hypnotized, make some small changes, and ultimately carve a new path for their lives.

There are, however, also HSPs who, sadly, miss out on this ideal moment. Especially while they are still young, many HSPs are not yet prepared to make meaningful adjustments to the plans they've made for their lives. They don't yet see that they are beginning to ENTANGLE themselves more and more in both internal and external circumstances. The immense effort required to continue to hold on to such incongruous concepts about life is not experienced as such, and the chains that encircle them grow ever tighter. The essential process of PERSONAL GROWTH becomes unnecessarily drawn out. Another phase of life emerges, one that initially hinders the direct path to awakening (from the hypnosis).

5.2 THE OVERLOAD PHASE

Things start to get harder and harder at work. You've long since gotten used to the knots in the muscles of your neck and back. Perhaps you're also suffering from joint pain (rheumatism) or gastrointestinal issues. If you're experiencing these sorts of vague complaints, or if you're having trouble sleeping, at the very least, this is an indication that your HES is trying to send you an important signal.

At this stage, you are using most your energy just to maintain the status quo. You are now trying with any means possible to control your life, so that you can still achieve all of your current ideas and plans.

You are sensing ever more clearly that you probably aren't going to be able to fall in line with the mainstream crowd after all. And yet, you still vehemently refuse to make any changes. Anything new seems threatening to you. You would rather put up with the current situation than to subject yourself to the nebulous perils of the unknown. You tell yourself that maybe somewhere, at some point, things will improve.

In this phase, the power of hope is what keeps you going.

Either you still truly believe in your career or you have already become a slave to the financial obligations you have ENTANGLED yourself in. You view a change in your professional situation as a threat to maintaining your social standing. Although you feel ever more distinctly that you are being robbed of your freedom, you don't see a way out. So, you just keep going.

You begin to notice how much more frequently you find yourself using the word "MUST".

The highly sensitive company boss, who for years now has stubbornly stuck to his original business concept, finds himself suffering from a loss in profits. He decides he needs to work even harder. He's already spoken for the umpteenth time with his bank. He let go of any semblance of pride and literally begged the bank officer to raise his credit limit one last time. He knows by now, though, that he won't be able to pay off his mountain of debt by sticking to his usual business practices. He begins to lie, cheat, and pull the wool over his customers' eyes. But now his highly developed conscience won't let him sleep. He finds himself hoping for a miracle.

Non-employed HSPs may visit a therapist and be told that their parents are to blame for everything. Something mysterious must certainly have happened during their childhood. Perhaps there was even sexual abuse, or their mother had secretly tried to have an abortion. Young parents who are HSPs are especially determined that they are going to do a much better job with their own children. They literally smother them with their performance mindsets and notions of what the PERFECT future would be. Rather than pursuing careers of their own, these parents make their children their substitute career. The children become a projection of the parent's own longings. Now it is the children who have to fit in with the mainstream. Children have desires instilled in them that are not their own.

What's more, they are put in a position of having to fulfill the need of their highly sensitive mother or father to be ACKNOWLEDGED. The children now begin to feel a subtle pressure being put on them by their highly sensitive parent. They sense clearly that ever more gratitude, love, and ACKNOWLEDGEMENT are being demanded of them. It may also be the case that the spouse or partner is called upon to provide the overloaded HSP with more ATTENTION. The children and other people in the lives of HSPs are now only being exploited as a supply of positive energy to help the HSP better cope with their own deadlocked situation.

Depending on the type of a situation you find yourself in, it's going to take a lot of courage in the OVERLOAD PHASE to still be able to LET GO. You will perceive everything that now happens as a step backwards or as a departure from your youthful dreams. And with every additional aspect that appears to deteriorate, your chances of experiencing a breakdown increase.

You are reaching the utmost limits
of your hypersensitivity.

You will definitely have become aware that you have changed for the worse. Glaring lights, certain noises, unpleasant odors and many other things will seem more irritating than ever before. You may even experience panic attacks or tinnitus. Many people attribute these symptoms solely to their high sensitivity. They are under the impression that all HSPs suffer from such symptoms. They don't want to believe that it is not their high sensitivity itself that is the problem, but rather their failure to live in accordance with their own nature.

At this point, many HSPs also begin to examine the issue of nutrition. Perhaps by eating the right foods, they can bring their bodies back into a symptom-free existence. However, all the time they spend thinking about what a healthy diet would entail further increases their degree of intellectualization. Many of them rediscover their favorite pastime of gathering extravagant amounts of knowledge. Nutritional guidance from other people – including marketing experts – works its way into their lives. Just the very desire to eat more healthily increases their degree of overload.

Last but not least, some HSPs discover their spiritual side – but here, too, they take only an *intellectual* approach to finding inner peace. Perhaps all they need to do to be able to fulfill their life's dreams is to think the right thoughts. Other begin to believe that they can manifest their desires through their minds alone. They start to organize their concepts about life around the universe, God, or someone or something else and hope through this to discover the perfect meditation technique. Under the heading of: *Maybe I just need to meditate more to improve my life.*

Topics related to spirituality provide a wonderful opportunity for delving more deeply into the philosophical aspects of life. Unfortunately, for many HSPs, this turns out to be the wrong path – at least in the OVERLOAD PHASE. More often than not, this simply increases the degree to which they are intellectualizing. This also leads to serious misunderstandings. They may use the wrong form of meditation, or they may place their hope in methods for predicting the future. This creates other, new forms of bondage. Some HSPs even go so far as to only do that which they have been advised to do by fortune tellers, astrologers, other gurus.

Other HSPs, on the other hand, travel to the Far East and return with a new name, not even aware that they are in bondage to the (foreign) energy field of the person who has given them this name. Yet others undergo spiritual initiations, become caught up in esoteric pyramid schemes, spend a small fortune on seminars, and slowly but surely lose their intellectual independence. Some even experience paranormal phenomena and come away completely impassioned. They now hope that angels, spirits, or even almighty God will put in a personal appearance and finally tell them what they need to do.

At the end of the day, HSPs completely lose their trust in their own thinking. What they are developing is the polar opposite of INHERENT TRUST, and the degree to which other people's thoughts and their own intellectualization determine their actions is reaching its zenith.

Incidentally, if you are also experiencing psychic phenomena, this should put you at the highest level of *red alert.* This would mean that your AES was just about to make direct contact with the INVISIBLE WORLD (rather than your HES). This means that the electromagnetic radiation in your head would have already reached such a dangerous level that electromagnetic induction was already taking place autonomously. You would already be so far off the ground that your entire body would be drifting off into the INVISIBLE WORLD (which is only meant to happen at the moment of death).

If you have ever been affected by one of the situations I have described, I can absolutely understand why. For example, people have always found paranormal effects fascinating – especially those people who are somewhat mentally unstable. I would like to remind you, though, that you will never be able to perceive the INVISIBLE WORLD through your normal senses (hearing, sight, smell, touch, etc.) Young HSPs, because of their lack of inner stability, are in particular danger of intercepting electromagnetic influences from foreign sources – and I don't even want to begin to imagine exactly what these might be.

By the way, this can also happen when people take mind-expanding drugs. As the name already suggests, these drugs *expand* the connections to your consciousness (AES/mind). They open the floodgates to foreign electromagnetic influences that you may never be able to get rid of. Doctors' offices are full of fragile patients who have taken hallucinogenic drugs and now are unable to rid themselves of their resultant psychoses. If you, too, think you want to *open* the door to psychic or drug-induced experiences, my advice to you is to leave it *closed*. Don't encourage these kinds of experiences. Your highly sensitive being is much too fragile for you to open yourself up to such potent influences.

Let's get back to the actual overload phase. If you ever find yourself sliding into it, you need to take immediate action to get out of it. The first thing to do is to free your head of any excess energy. Anything that requires you to move your arms or legs is ideal for this first step.

Physical activity and sweating are standard GROUNDING METHODS and are an easy way to achieve this. They also reduce the number of stress hormones in your system – and during the OVERLOAD PHASE, your body is simply flooded with these. This is an especially important aspect, since when your body is in hormonal emergency mode, this also significantly weakens your immune system. When you're already on overload, the last thing you need is to open the door to every virus and bacteria that comes along – not to even mention the danger that your adrenal system could simply shut down completely (see, e.g., *Adrenal Fatigue: The 21st Century Stress Syndrome, by James L. Wilson*).

You should also attempt to regularly shut out as many external stimuli as possible. This includes everything that your senses transmit to your brain. Soft lighting, soft, loose clothing, avoiding strong scents, and above all, absolute quiet is what is called for. Ear plugs can sometimes work wonders (if you can get used to them). The more you can isolate your senses from the external world, the faster your brain can recover.

Even though at this point it will be far more difficult to put the advice in the chapter on LETTING GO into practice, unfortunately, you don't have any other choice. What makes it even more difficult is that now, at this advanced stage of your intellectual development, the probability is exceedingly high that you may even be faced with major upheavals in your life. If you still have a choice about how to approach the changes that are now imminent, I would advise you to proceed with great caution:

To the best of your ability, avoid making any hard breaks.

To this day, I have only rarely encountered people who would say in retrospect that the sudden, self-induced major changes they made really needed to happen. Without exception, they report that they actually went from the frying pan into the fire. It would be far better for you if you could somehow attempt to find a middle ground.

I have, however, also encountered HSPs who, despite overwhelming symptoms of being overloaded, stubbornly refused to even consider the idea of LETTING GO. Some even developed a kind of pathological obstinacy. They are willing to go to the utmost extremes simply to maintain the status quo. They continually and massively torpedo their own PERSONAL GROWTH. And this leads to yet another phase of life, one which should have been avoidable. It creates another extreme.

5.3 THE LIFE-NEGATING PHASE

Don't worry! You are reading this book and that means that you are definitely not in this terrible phase. I can assure you, that you have already masterfully conquered the lion's share of your emotional challenges. If this weren't true, you would be mentally ill and not capable of reading a book. You would have lost any ability to concentrate on anything. You, however, are indeed able to concentrate on the words in this book (ADULT EGO STATE), to experience feelings as you do so (NEWBORN EGO STATE), and to be aware of the "Aha!" effect (HIGHER EGO STATE). Perhaps you are even approaching the finish line in finding your vocational calling. I would still like to briefly discuss this phase because it obviously belongs to our topic. It is notable that many HSPs are definitely very familiar with thoughts of ending their lives.

In general, HSPs who have lost their zest for life have not succeeded in resolving the worries of their NES. This leads them to completely shut down emotionally, leaving them with only their intellect. The last emotions they experience are, without exception, old feelings from the past that have been stored in their brains. In the end, they are unable to summon up real emotions about anything.

They act as though they experience deep and painful emotions but fail to realize that these are never about the present moment. Emotionally, they merely struggle with feelings they have had in the past or make emotional projections of the future. They are unable to experience the present moment on an emotional level and, sadly, only perceive it intellectually. They can only process their surrounding on a cognitive level.

These distraught people have completely lost contact with their intuition. Not even the slightest bit of information from their HES can be perceived by their AES. The result is a string of bad luck, feelings of bitterness, even a complete loss of direction in life. The protective force of the body's own intuition no longer functions. There is little hope that these people will be able to start the PERSONAL GROWTH process by themselves.

The world has apparently reached such a degree of emotional brutality that for some HSPs, it seems impossible that they will ever be able to conquer their PRIMAL FEARS on their own. This saddens me deeply. I hope that you will never find yourself sinking into such a phase. If this happens, however, there is only one way out: You must AWAKEN from your hypnotic state (in this specific case, please do this only under the care of a medical professional and *not* with the help of gurus, influencers, life coaches, annual subscriptions to motivational speakers, social media groups, chat rooms, or anything of the sort!)

5.4 THE AWAKENING PHASE

The sooner you rid yourself of concepts about life that were never yours to begin with, the longer you will have to enjoy life to the maximum. Basically, at some point, it will be as though the scales fall from your eyes, and you will see that you have actually never lived your life the way you were intended to live it. It will seem almost shocking when you realize that, up until now, you have simply been busy trying to suppress your PRIMAL FEARS or striving to be ACKNOWLEDGED.

In this AWAKENING PHASE, you will tell the mainstream to get lost. What's more, you will also begin to appreciate your highly sensitive being – with all its quirks, needs, and ingenious gifts.

Depending on how difficult it has been for you to cope with your high sensitivity so far, in this phase, you may still have some baggage from your past to dispose of (major upheavals, dependencies, the wrong circle of friends, etc.) You will see that some of that upheaval wasn't even necessary. Or you may realize that one crisis or another actually put you back on the right path.

Above all, however, one of your primary strengths will now begin to emerge. You will begin to better UNDERSTAND not only yourself, but, first and foremost, the others around you. This includes not only the people currently in your life, but, in particular, those from the past. In the process, you will be able to come to terms with many of the grudges you may have held in the past (*my mother or my father couldn't help the way things were – she/he was highly sensitive too ...*).

Now, in this phase, you are going to take enormous steps forward in your development. You will still have to deal with the issues involved in LETTING GO, but your sense of inner peace and freedom from anxiety will increase more and more.

Once you have finally found the middle ground in all of the aspects of LETTING GO (*taking breaks, external stimuli, the mainstream, your income, your attitude toward your job, self-centeredness, self-promotion, sources of stress*), you will begin to experience magical moments more and more often. Answers, insights, and many "Aha!" moments will seemingly appear out of nowhere. The changes taking place in your environment will let you know that your HES is now functioning at full power. Now you can experience first-hand what it means to possess powerful intuitive talents.

Now, it is especially important to focus more on your sleeping habits. Your brain now perceives far more clearly the volume of information coming from your HES.

Now you will finally begin to regulate your life while you sleep.

This last statement is fundamentally important for you. Shoo away your AES, with its lust for control and desire to meddle in your future. Only your HES regulates your future. You – that is, your AES – have only one single task:

During the day, you must put into practice whatever ideas you had as you awoke that morning.

Right after you awake in the morning, your mind will be full of insights, answers, or other ideas. During the night, your HES has downloaded practically every bit of information you need. Your Wi-Fi connection to the INVISIBLE WORLD is now functioning perfectly:

Don't make important decisions until
you have slept on them overnight.

Go ahead and take the term AWAKENING PHASE literally. Instead of spending time brooding over something, just wait until you AWAKEN the next morning.

If you take this to heart, and if you have been successful in your earlier LETTING GO efforts, then your long-standing mental struggles will finally come to an end. In their place, you will notice a comforting inner surrender to your destiny (your intuition) and, above all, to your future. Humility, insight, and a new range of emotions will now come especially easily to you. At the same time, your excessive earnestness will be replaced by generosity, tolerance, serenity, and, above all, the ability to laugh at yourself. Life will become more and more beautiful.

Now is also the time when you will come across your vocational calling. In doing so, you will be confronted with yet another mysterious magical power your intuition possesses:

In actuality, you are not searching for your calling –
your calling is searching for you.

When the time is ripe, as if by magic, the right solutions, coincidences, and ideas will come to you, leaving you with goosebumps and a sense of disbelief. You will be at the right place at the right time, meeting the right people. Closed doors will belong to the distant past and you will be able to immediately recognize which ones are open.

This experience, where the most wildly different pieces of the mosaic suddenly come together to form a picture of your vocational path, will be a decisive event in your life. Anyone who has ever been privileged to experience such a magical moment will never forget it.

Until then, there is just one thing you have to do. You need to train yourself to have a certain mindfulness with regard to your surroundings. You must become more attentive since, in the end, your intuition will lead you exactly where you need to be. You need to be listening when opportunity knocks. To be sure you are doing this, it is crucial that you keep in mind the general definition of your calling from the last chapter. To repeat:

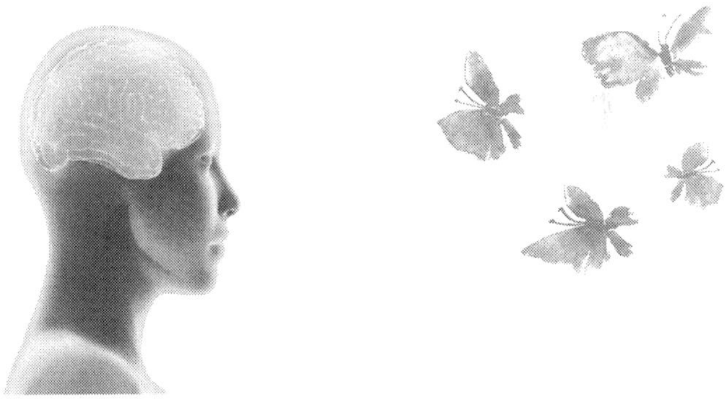

You want to develop something of your own that improves or enriches the lives of others.

Learn this by heart!

The best thing to do is to write this on a piece of paper and hang it on your bathroom mirror (next to that other note). Once these words are firmly etched in your memory, you will be fully prepared for those moments when favorable circumstances and pointers for your vocational calling suddenly appear in front of you. You'll be better able to identify people, situations, and places that you so urgently need for fulfilling your professional (as well as private) hopes and desires.

Even if you still really enjoy your alone time, at this stage, you should still seek out face-to-face conversations more frequently. This will not only lead to even more lucky coincidences and helpful pointers, but you will also be able to broaden and further differentiate your range of emotional reactions.

From this point on, be open to meeting new people.

And please listen attentively to others. What's more, pay attention to people you may not even know yet. These people often blurt out something that fits in perfectly with your situation. Train yourself to recognize these magical kinds of moments. They will be the key to your future. Only if you are open to new experiences will you create the right conditions for finding those open doors, and then, you simply have to step through them. *You* are no longer the one who must constantly play the role of the guardian angel – others are going to take on that role for you. *You* are now the one who reaps the benefits.

Incidentally, beware, too, of your own preconceptions about who these people might be. You will be amazed to see that it is precisely those people whom, in the past, you would normally have overlooked. The more aloof people (usually HSPs), in particular, are the ones who hold the key to your situation (without even knowing it themselves).

Be alert to the people with whom you cross paths.

Just as this book coincidentally made its way into your hands, new circumstances and new people are also going to enter your life. As I've already said, your HES really has your best interests at heart. You will come to truly understand this during this AWAKENING PHASE, perhaps for the first time in your life.

Finally, I want to provide you with a couple of tools that will allow you to better evaluate whether or not something is truly related to your vocational calling. This is probably not really necessary, since by this point, you are in possession of a highly functioning intuition. Still, better safe than sorry.

Think back on what you've learned: When you improve or enrich the lives of others, you also improve and enrich your own life. This means that once you have LET GO, you will no longer have to be worried about your highly sensitive existence.

The willingness to UNDERSTAND and fulfill the desires of others leads to yet another fantastic benefit for HSPs:

Your vocational calling will always
take care of your financial needs.

In practical terms, this is a business model you enter into with your own intuition. When you take care of the needs of others (enrich and improve), this will always come back to you in material form – revenue, a salary, or some other tangible means that provides you with financial security.

The reverse is also true, however. If you are presented with an opportunity that doesn't, at a minimum, allow you to keep an adequate roof over your head and put food on your table (once you have adopted the principles of avoiding mad consumerism), this is always a sign that this opportunity has nothing to do with your true vocational calling. The aspect of securing your existence not only corresponds to a primal evolutionary principle, but, at the same time, can be used as your highly sensitive control test as you search for your vocational calling.

Beyond this, there is also another concrete method for easily evaluating whether a professional opportunity or your current job are right for you or not.

If you find yourself struggling too hard,
you are usually on the wrong path.

Of course, when I use the word *struggling*, I don't mean it in a physical sense. It goes without saying that you can't just sit home and wait for something to happen. A certain amount of effort, activity, courage, and a great willingness to change are obviously necessary. What I'm talking about when I say *struggling too hard* are the unresolvable conflicts – when something just won't work out, stumbling blocks keep popping up, or you run into a dead end.

When something just doesn't seem to flow easily,
this is often an indication of a CLOSED DOOR.

If, in this situation, someone tries to convince you that you simply have to set some goals and then blindly follow them, no matter what, then this is the wrong approach – at least for you. What you are then dealing with is a more pernicious form of motivation (being motivated by a perspective that doesn't actually exist). Either that or you happen to be sitting at the movies, watching a Hollywood film that once again stirs up desires in you that were never actually your own.

Since all good things come in threes, here is a third option for easily assessing whether or not you have already fully entered the AWAKENING PHASE:

If you are still having nightmares, you are coming
into contact during the day with things that don't
belong to your vocational calling.

Of course, all of us have bad dreams from time to time. If you notice that you are having nightmares increasingly frequently, however, this is a typical indication that you have not yet completely LET GO.

Somewhere in your life, there is still a strong conflict that you haven't yet been able to resolve or that you haven't yet accepted, because it can't be resolved anyway. It is also possible that there is a certain conflict in your life that you aren't even aware of yet.

The only thing that can prevent your HES from functioning properly is an existing conflict – whether internal or external. Ultimately, certain PRIMAL FEARS are always responsible for conflicts not being able to be resolved. And fears are well-known to be toxic to an INTUITIVELY LED LIFE. If you find yourself in a phase where you are having nightmares and you are also being confronted with a potential vocational calling, you can bet that the whole thing has nothing to do with you yet. You must then go back to the chapter on LETTING GO and work your way through it again. And you have to keep doing this until the majority of these bad dreams have disappeared.

Let's briefly pull all of this together. All in all, you have three simple tools at your disposal that will allow you to easily assess whether your vocational calling has already emerged:

1. Your vocational calling will provide you with adequate material reward.
2. If it is your true vocational calling, things will flow smoothly, and you won't constantly be running into roadblocks.
3. You will never find your vocational calling during phases where you are plagued by nightmares.

All in all, during the AWAKENING PHASE, you will certainly experience a roller coaster of different emotions. Moments of speechlessness will alternately give way to moments of happy confusion.

There will be simply too many new (and mysterious) impressions and insights for you to just sit back calmly and observe with them. Experiencing just how an INTUITIVELY LED LIFE is the key to your happiness will certainly be a breathtaking experience for you.

Unfortunately, however, you will also begin to have to walk a fine line:

The delicate little flower of
AWAKENING is very fragile.

Following those first euphoric experiences with your intuition and the many new positive experiences with LETTING GO, you are going to feel as though you hold the divine golden key to the universe in your hands. Yes, at times, you may even feel as though you yourself are God. This will not only give you goosebumps, but it can also put you in a new and dangerous situation – very quickly, you may abandon the humility, modesty, and sense of groundedness you have achieved:

Arrogance and hubris are lying in wait for you.

You could very quickly fall back into old patterns of behavior. You'll hear yourself thinking that perhaps those old goals for your life (the ones that came from outside you) are possible after all. *After all, now I know how the whole thing works.*

Such backsliding can rapidly destroy everything you've achieved, however. I know what I'm talking about here – I've gone around in circles like this a few times myself. Following the AWAKENING PHASE, I repeatedly fell back into my old patterns of behavior. This put me back into my intellectualized mindset and I ultimately allowed myself to once again become overwhelmed, etc., etc.

You will keep going around in circles until you have completely, one-hundred-percent, awakened from your hypnotic state, when all of your insights have been fully integrated into your life and you are standing with both feet firmly on the ground. Then, LIBERATION is beckoning.

5.5 THE LIBERATION PHASE

Actually, this phase in your personal development is no longer related to the topic of your VOCATIONAL CALLING. It has more to do with your PURPOSE.

As I mentioned earlier, in the search for your vocational calling, it isn't necessarily important to discuss all of the phases that come after the awakening phase. I would still, however, like to briefly describe the LIBERATION PHASE, because I would never want to withhold from you the fact that something truly *heart*felt may await you.

The LIBERATION PHASE represents a process that goes by relatively unnoticed, in the background, as it were. You can't consciously bring about this GROWTH spurt. It's much more likely that you will be occupied with issues around LETTING GO and AWAKENING. And the tasks you have taken on as you begin to carry out your vocational calling will also mean that your thoughts are elsewhere.

The work you are now doing is very fulfilling professionally. Every evening, you look forward to the next day. You know what needs to be done and you get back more energy from your work than you put into it.

You begin to discover that you enjoy working. You no longer have the feeling that you are sacrificing your free time to your job. Your private life and your professional life begin to merge. It becomes more and more difficult to determine what part of what you are doing still counts as work and what has already become part of your free-time activities.

You're no longer working at a job just so that you can afford to go on vacation and get away from it. In short:

You have found your place
in the professional world.

Your agonizing search is now over. You KNOW that what you are doing is right and is a natural part of your life. And if changes need to be made, then you also KNOW that your intuition will not only make you aware of this early on but will also unmistakably guide you to your new path (those open and closed doors).

At some point though, there will come a very special moment in which you will, for the first time, experience something that, up until now, you have never known. And at this moment, your *heart* will play the leading role.

If you take a look at your body, you will observe that your chest is located practically midway between your head (intellect) and your stomach (emotions). And this is where your heart resides. It is not only your body's engine; it is also the source of your vitality. Even cancer cannot penetrate this sacred space. Only in the rarest of cases have malignant cancer cells been known to attack the heart. Almost never do even the most hostile of these cells succeed in harming this powerful source of our life force.

In addition, the heart is an organ that is not dependent on the brain in order to carry out its function. Like your brain, it also possesses nerve cells, but in today's medical terminology, it is characterized as an independent sensory organ. As long as it is supplied with glucose, it is capable of beating on its own, even when it is outside the body. You could actually stick it in a container and watch as, disconnected from your brain, it continued to pump away. The heart is autonomous. A site of independence. A symbol of absolute freedom.

Many people believe that the heart is the seat of love. And it is. However, this includes not only the love of other people, but, and especially, the love of life. The heart possesses the strongest electrical power of all the organs in our body. This power is approximately sixty times stronger than the electrical signals from our brains. The heart's magnetic field is a whopping five thousand times stronger (see, e.g., *Rollin McCraty, Ph.D., Institute of Heart Math, Boulder Creek, California, USA*).

Once you have freed your heart from all PRIMAL FEARS through the LETTING GO process, it will suddenly revive (the feeling of "*that's a weight off my chest*").

Once that weight is off your chest – that is, your heart – you will sense an indescribable feeling of unconditional, all-encompassing love for life itself. It's something you could never put into words. When you experience this moment of joy and freedom for the first time, you will KNOW that this is LIBERATION. Tears will flow from your eyes. All of the negative drama from earlier in your life will rise up and evaporate forever. You will have now reached your goal:

Your fragile NEWBORN EGO STATE has finally grown into a joyful INNER CHILD.

This is the LIBERATION of your NES! You will quickly realize that the only purpose all of the phases of your PERSONAL GROWTH served was to restore the connection between your intellect and your emotions. Your thoughts and your feelings are now again one – joined together in your heart.

Once you have experienced the magic and the power of your heart for the first time, you will immediately understand that it was never necessary to have a purpose in life. Your longing to find purpose was simply a sly trick played on you by your intellect (your AES). No, what you have been so urgently yearning for your entire life is something completely different:

What you were always searching for
was a passion for life.

It now turns out that you were wrong about everything that you thought, up until now, came from your heart. You become aware that you have never truly felt it before. Everything you have been striving for until now was a product of your mind's hypnosis.

At this dramatic moment of LIBERATION, you arrive at a new stage in your PERSONAL GROWTH. This indescribable feeling – a deep passion for life and infinite freedom – makes you forget any fears about the future. You no longer need to turn to gurus, fortune tellers, or anyone else to give you advice. You stop asking others for answers to existential questions. From now on, your new INHERENT TRUST will supply you with CERTAINTY.

Your urgent need for gratitude, attention, and acknowledgement seems to vanish into thin air. You no longer need this sort of affirmation of love in your life. Instead, you have discovered a new type of love. This is what, from now on, will be your great passion. The vibration of a type of love that can never be experienced between humans. You now love life itself and you can sense that life itself loves you, too.

For the first time, you experience
the feeling of TRUE SELF-LOVE.

Your PRIMAL FEARS have been banished by your new INHERENT TRUST. Your heart has been freed and can finally assume its original purpose. Your intuition, now fully awakened, lets you know immediately that from now on, everything you carry in your heart will also come to fruition.

You will be infinitely grateful for the path life has led you on so far, because all of the drama, blows of fate, and conflicts will seem like an almost ridiculously small sacrifice in comparison to that which you now hold in your hands.

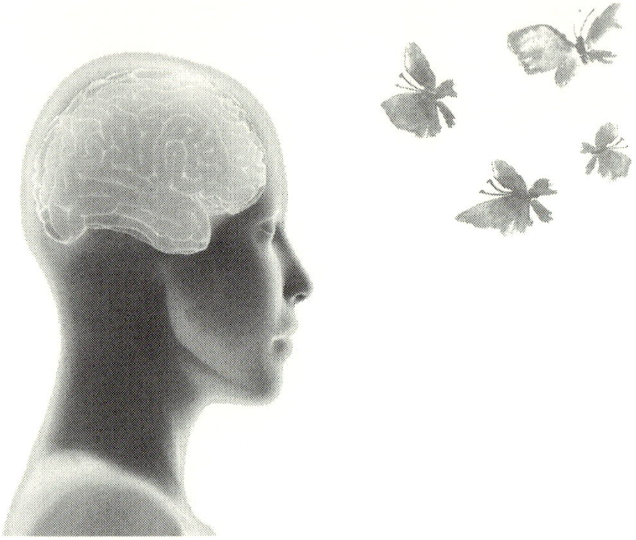

You have discovered
the magical power of being
a highly sensitive person!

Luca Rohleder

www.hochsensibilitaet-netzwerk.com

Made in the USA
Monee, IL
26 March 2022

93584898R00132